WE
SIGNED AWAY OUR LIVES

HOW ONE FAMILY GAVE EVERYTHING FOR THE GOSPEL

Kari Torjesen Malcolm

INTERVARSITY PRESS
DOWNERS GROVE, ILLINOIS 60515

InterVarsity Press is the book-publishing division of InterVarsity Christian Fellowship, a student movement active on campus at hundreds of universities, colleges and schools of nursing. For information about local and regional activities, write Public Relations Dept., InterVarsity Christian Fellowship, 6400 Schroeder Rd., P.O. Box 7895, Madison, WI 53707-7895.

All Scripture quotations, unless otherwise indicated, are from the Holy Bible, New International Version. Copyright © 1973, 1978, International Bible Society. Used by permission of Zondervan Bible Publishers.

Cover illustration: Greg Wray

ISBN 0-8308-1718-2

Printed in the United States of America

Library of Congress Cataloging-in-Publication Data

Malcolm, Kari Torjesen, 1925-
    We signed away our lives/Kari Malcolm.
      p.   cm.
    ISBN 0-8308-1718-2
    1. Torjesen family.   2. Malcolm family.   3. Missionaries—China—
Biography.   4. Missionaries—Norway—Biography.   5. Missionaries—
United States—Biography.   I. Title.
    BV3427.A1M34   1990
    266'.0092'2—dc20
    [B]   90-38692
                                                      CIP

| 12 | 11 | 10 | 9 | 8 | 7 | 6 | 5 | 4 | 3 | 2 | 1 |
| 99 | 98 | 97 | 96 | 95 | 94 | 93 | 92 | 91 | 90 |

To Peter and Valborg Torjesen's
fourteen grandchildren,
to whom this story
of God's goodness and faithfulness belongs:

Leif Peter, Paul, Ruth, John, Finn and Jean Valborg
(Edvard and Jenny's children)

Kirsten and Lois
(Kari and Bob's children)

Erik Peter, Kristine, Malika and Mark
(Hakon and Karen's children)

Hild and Rolf
(Torje and Reidun's children)

. . . we will tell the next generation
the praiseworthy deeds of the LORD,
his power, and the wonders he has done. . . .
so the next generation would know them,
even the children yet to be born,
and they in turn would tell their children.
Then they would put their trust in God
and would not forget his deeds
but would keep his commands.
—Ps 78:4, 6, 7

1 Blood Rather Than Dollars *11*

2 Call to China *23*

3 Newlyweds Pioneer in Hequ *35*

4 The Song of the River Calls Us Home *49*

5 Peaceful Furlough in Norway *67*

6 War in China *79*

7 No Cost Is Too Great *103*

8 Life Goes On *117*

9 Pearl Harbor and Prison Camp *135*

10 Far's and Mor's Ministry to Mongols and Chinese Continues *155*

Postlude *169*

Appendix 1 *178*

Appendix 2 *179*

Chronology of Events *180*

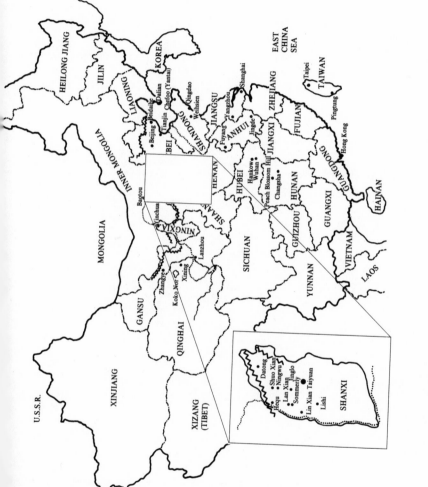

U.S.S.R.

MONGOLIA

HEILONG JIANG

JILIN

INNER MONGOLIA

KOREA

LIAONING

Beijing • Beidaihe
• Tianjin • Dalian
HEBEI • Chefoo (Yantai)
SHANDONG
• Qingdao
• Weihsien
Yangzhou • Shanghai
JIANGSU
Fuyang • ANHUI
HENAN Jingde
• Hankow
HUBEI • Wuhan
Peach Blossom Hill
Changsha •
HUNAN
Baotou •
Yinchuan •
NINGXIA
SHAANXI
Lanzhou •
Zhangye • Koko Nor
Xining •
QINGHAI

XINJIANG

GANSU

XIZANG
(TIBET)

SICHUAN

GUIZHOU

YUNNAN

GUANGXI

GUANGDONG

VIETNAM

LAOS

HAINAN

Hong Kong

ZHEJIANG

FUJIAN

JIANGXI

EAST
CHINA
SEA

Taipei •
TAIWAN
Pingtung

SHANXI inset:

Datong •
Shuo Xian •
Hequ • • Ningwu
Lan Xian • • Jingle
• Sommerly
Lishi • Jin Xian Taiyuan

SHANXI

∧∧∧∧ Great Wall
——— Provincial Borders
·········· Yellow River

Blood Rather Than Dollars

1

"You are not tourists," Dr. Zhang said emphatically, "so I will tell the provincial authorities not to treat you as tourists. I shall tell them you are a son and a daughter of the city who want to come home."

During dinner my brother Hakon asked Dr. Zhang, from Shanxi Province, "Have you ever heard of Hequ?" To his surprise he got an affirmative answer.

"I haven't only heard of it," Dr. Zhang said. "It is part of my medical territory." Soon she was promising both Hakon and me that she would work diligently to get us home to Hequ—where we grew up as children—even if the city was officially "closed."

I had been planning to go home to Hequ from the minute China reopened its door to foreigners in the late seventies. Whenever I met

Chinese students I would ask if they had heard of Hequ. Nobody had. But maybe that wasn't so surprising, since my missionary parents did ask to go to a place where there was no gospel witness and where nobody else wanted to go.

Hequ was one of the most remote places in Shanxi. It was the gateway to Inner Mongolia, where the foreboding desert lay before any brave traveler. A city of 10,000 people, its citizens were among the poorest and least educated in all of China. But that's where my father asked to go in 1921. Now, sitting with Dr. Zhang and my brother, I chuckled that decisions made so long ago continued to affect us in the 1980s.

For there was one crucial problem with going to Hequ. As Dr. Zhang had indicated, it was not an "open city." Chinese embassies around the world gave maps to tourists wanting to visit China, maps clearly marking the open cities. That meant you needn't ask about going to a closed city. But God had an "angel" prepared to help us.

Dr. Zhang, a pediatrician from Shanxi, came to the University of Minnesota in 1987 to visit her son who was in a Ph.D. program. She soon met Carol Hone, a volunteer teacher who had helped her son improve his English skills. Carol wanted Dr. Zhang to meet my brother Hakon whom she knew came from Shanxi, the same province as Dr. Zhang, and his wife, Karen—a pediatrician—from the same profession. After they all met, Hakon called me to get me in on this exciting Shanxi connection. Without Carol we wouldn't have met Dr. Zhang, and without Dr. Zhang we could not have returned to Hequ. God's "angel" made our going home possible. After Dr. Zhang returned to Shanxi, she worked for our permits to visit our hometown, and soon the dates were set for my husband and me, and Hakon and Karen to go to Hequ in 1988.

Anticipation Mingles with Memories
Anticipation grew each month as we moved closer to our journey to

Hequ. I had lots of questions after all the years of no contact. Would our many friends there, those who would remember us, still be around? Would the church my parents founded be there? Would the Christians feel free to come and talk to us? And would we be able to find my father's grave?

During the long years of silence when we had had no contact with our brothers and sisters in China, I often thought of the silent message spoken by the graves of foreigners. Our family had two graves in China—my father's in Hequ, and my nephew David's in Lanzhou, Gansu. I wondered what unspoken sentiments went through the residents' minds as they passed those two graves.

Such thoughts were intensified in 1986 when I visited one of the last of my parents' Shanxi colleagues. Tante Signe, a single woman, was living in the home for retired missionaries in Oslo, Norway. When I stopped in to see her, she wasted no time on small talk:

"Imagine the honor and privilege that was mine to go to China," she said with her eyes glowing. Her mind and spirit were clearly not in the present in a wrinkled body—well over eighty—but in the great adventure of her past as a missionary.

"Imagine, Kari," she said, "I was just an ordinary young girl in Norway, in my early twenties with nurse's training and Bible school, but God called me to China. I was so awed when God called me, that a nobody like me could be of service in the Kingdom.

"Come closer, Kari, I have something very important to tell you," she continued, leaning toward me as I sat by her bedside. I had heard it before, but on each visit my heart throbbed to hear that wonderful story again.

She didn't say a word about why her arm was in a sling, or why she was confined to bed. A visit from someone interested in her past in China was too precious to waste on a litany of aches and pains. Instead, she shared with me again the primary purpose for which she was born—not to conceive and mother a family, but to have a tiny part in the huge plan of God for the evangelization of China.

"Then I went to England for my training with the China Inland Mission [CIM]. There I had to sign a paper that I was willing to go to China and die for Jesus like so many martyrs before me. Jesus was worthy of my life and my death and so I signed willingly, thinking I would never return to Norway. I fully expected to die like your father did, having the honor to live and to die for Jesus."

I have always left Tante Signe with gratitude for the heritage given us by our parents and their colleagues. In our childhood in China the honor of living and dying for Jesus was held up to us as the highest calling for a pilgrim. To be totally available to the Captain of our salvation, to be sent anywhere on the spiritual battlefront, not holding back any personal aspirations or considerations, was the goal to be sought and admired. The missionaries of my parents' era had a vision of the kingdom that went well beyond themselves.

The Guiding Principle of My Parents' Lives

This world view was summed up for my parents in the truth of Philippians 1:20: "According to my earnest expectation and my hope, that in nothing I shall be ashamed, but that with all boldness, as always, so now also Christ shall be magnified in my body, whether it be by life, or by death" (KJV). We have the Bible my father took with him on his first journey to China. Beside this verse he has written in a neat hand, "MOTTO FOR CHINA, 1918."

This verse is the theme of this story because it became the guiding principle of my parents' lives. To them the Philippians passage meant Jesus was worth living and dying for. And yet they didn't talk much about it. Conversations around the table in our home and the homes of other missionaries were always joyful. There was the excitement of being pioneers in a new and shared venture for the gospel, and there was often a funny side to the story. For instance, we were sometimes received as spirits from another world. Some Chinese touched us to see if we were real. One woman, after she was sure my mother was real, lifted Mother's long skirt slightly to see what she wore underneath. When she saw a pink silk slip she protested, "But you should wear that on the outside." The minor conflicts of culture—when there was no danger of belittling the people we had come to serve—always provided something to laugh about.

On the other hand, when the missionaries prayed, "Thy Kingdom come, Thy will be done on earth as it is in heaven," it was no joke. For my parents this prayer meant the kingdom might come to China at the cost of their lives—and even the lives of their children. The Boxer Rebellion, an uprising against foreigners and Chinese Christians in 1900, resulted in the deaths of 189 missionaries, including 52 children. The memories of these massacres were still fresh when my father and mother arrived in Shanxi.

Indeed, of all the provinces in China, Shanxi suffered the most during the Boxer Rebellion. It had 159 foreign martyrs, the vast majority of the 189 killed in the Rebellion. But the crisis passed, with the calm words of a white-haired Shanxi pastor coming true. "Kingdoms may perish," he said with almost his last breath, "but the church of Christ can never be destroyed."

Preparing the Church for Persecution
Such confidence in God and willingness for martyrdom was passed on to the church in China. The missionaries had no way of knowing that China would be closed to missionaries after 1949, nor did they have any inkling of the drastic changes that would take place after Chairman Mao assumed control. But in God's providence they gave the Chinese Christians the training they needed to live and die for Jesus Christ. Unwittingly they were telling them what John was instructed

to relay to the persecuted church of Smyrna: "Do not be afraid of what you are about to suffer. . . . Be faithful, even to the point of death, and I will give you the crown of life" (Rev 2:10).

Through their deaths some, like my father, had been an example of the highest expression of unconditional love, for Jesus said, "Greater love has no one than this, that he lay down his life for his friends" (Jn 15:13). Others, like my mother, went through the pain of seeing the door to China closed, never to be allowed to go back and show love for the people to whom they had devoted their lives.

But in spite of all the disappointment involved in the ouster from China (many missionaries were at the height of their careers), these 8,000 men and women were a unique and privileged group. None of them knew this at the time, and so were unconscious of the very important role they were playing—actually preparing the Chinese church for the Communist revolution and the persecution it would bring.

But what if they had known? Would it have made a difference if that generation of China missionaries had known what was just around the corner? I don't know. But if in God's providence the missionaries didn't know the future, then also in God's providence they brought about the will of the kingdom even without knowing the significance of what they were doing.

This releases me from the danger of idealizing my parents' generation of missionaries. I do not want to write a hagiography, but I want to write the story of 8,000 missionaries who had a unique place in history. They were all sinners, facing the same temptations as the rest of us (1 Cor 10:13). Among them there were those who should never have been sent overseas, but somehow were caught in the spirit of the time and wanted a part in evangelizing China. Many missionaries were also trapped in the colonial mentality of that time. So it is not the story of a perfect group of missionaries I am telling, but of some imperfect people who were penetrated by God's grace to meet the need of the hour.

One Story That Tells Many

As I tell the story of one family, my family, I am also telling the untold stories of the majority of the missionaries in China in the decades before Chairman Mao. Since they didn't know the importance of their roles, nor those reporting on missions in China at that time, I am left with a sense of divine compulsion to tell the story of some ordinary people who did an extraordinary job.

All the 1,300 missionaries with the China Inland Mission had signed a commitment to be willing to die in China. I remember well when the martyrdom of John and Betty Stam shook the mission and the entire Christian world. Both had been uniquely prepared to lay down their lives. Betty arrived in China ahead of John, and after language school was assigned to Fuyang, Anhui. Before she got there in 1932, a senior missionary had been captured and carried into the mountains by Red bandits. No one has since heard from him. Thus Betty faced the possibility of death.

John's preparation came through a poem sent to him at language school, written about the death of another missionary at the hands of bandits in North China. When gun in hand, they asked their prisoner if he was afraid, he answered, "No. If you shoot, I go straight to heaven." The poem about this martyrdom, written by China missionary E. H. Hamilton, meant much to John Stam:

Afraid? Of what?
Afraid to see the Savior's face,
To hear His welcome, and to trace
The glory gleam from wounds of grace?
Afraid—of that?

Afraid? Of what?
A flash, a crash, a pierced heart;
Darkness, light, O Heaven's art!
A wound of his counterpart!
Afraid—of that?

Afraid? Of what?
To do by death what life could not—
Baptize with blood a stony plot,
Till souls shall blossom from the spot?
Afraid—of that?

John and Betty were ready to "baptize with blood a stony plot, till souls shall blossom from the spot." It happened during the Long March of the Red Army to northwest China, an event famous for the army's bravery and heroism, as well as the suffering it inflicted on the civilian population. The Stams and their baby girl had just settled in their new assignment when a Red unit attacked their city and the Stams were captured. Early the next day (December 7, 1934) John and Betty knelt side by side and were beheaded. A Christian doctor who did his best to plead for their lives joined them in their martyrdom. The baby was miraculously overlooked and rescued by Chinese Christians.

When John and Betty were executed, the Sixth Red Army had already moved into Guizhou Province and captured two more CIM missionaries as "spies for an imperialist government." They were forced to join the Long March. I remember praying for their rescue as a little girl. When one was released after 413 days of captivity, the other's parting words to him were, "Pray that I may recklessly preach Christ." And he did, until he was released after a few more months of captivity.

In those troubled years before and after the Japanese invasion, all missionaries and their families knew that dying for Jesus was a real possibility. And so the missionaries' own commitment to give their lives qualified them to pass on such a commitment to the Chinese Christians, many of whom faced greater persecution after the Revolution than their spiritual mentors ever had.

Daredevils for Christ

Friends often ask me how we could live on the razor edge of danger year after year and not get depressed. But remember that my parents and their colleagues were caught up in the kingdom where God was the center. This released them from self-centered preoccupation with their own survival. Personal fulfillment or safety was a by-product, not a goal, in their vision. Suffering was taken for granted and not something to avoid at all costs. As one of my parent's colleagues told me, "We were daredevils for Christ. We never thought of evacuating. We were too excited about the job we had to do."

And he said it with a hearty laugh. I can't think of a group of people who joked so much or laughed so much over life's complexities. There was a holy joy present in missionary gatherings, that fierce joy of knowing one is doing the right thing and God is pleased.

"I loved to hear your father tell stories," the old veteran missionary continued. "You see, he laughed so heartily in the process. He'd tell us about one of the eccentric characters from his hometown, Kristiansand, and we were right back there with him. He was never heavy-hearted. Strong convictions, yes, and serious about them, but always lots of fun."

Mother, whom we as Norwegians called Mor, had her own way of showing joy. Her first day in China (January 17, 1921) she could not sleep all night because she was so overjoyed that she had reached her destination. She wrote home, "God's goodness to me was so overwhelming that I just lay there hour after hour and just praised and

19

thanked my heavenly Father. . . . Imagine, I'm in China, the land of promise!"

Such joy was mixed with Mor's sense of destiny. She felt it was an honor and privilege to be called to the evangelization of China. With the holy joy of such a high calling, depression and anxiety about the possibility of death were held at bay. Nor were Mor and her colleagues likely to allow the trivia of life to preoccupy them. Instead, they took seriously Jesus' question, "Is not life more important than food, and the body more important than clothes?" (Mt 6:25).

In the area of material possessions my parents were further released by the CIM policy that did not obligate missionaries to raise their own support. Missionaries prayed for God to send in the funds, but didn't make those needs known publicly. What came in to the mission treasury was divided evenly among the missionaries, resulting in lean months and months of plenty. And with the simple lifestyle of those days of almost no equipment and few clothes, it was much easier to concentrate on why they were in China.

Such an outlook also affected the perception of missions. Too often today, missions is equated simply with money, or a local church's missionary budget, instead of with warm bodies from the pews who hear the call of God to go and make disciples of all nations. It is much easier to raise money than to challenge Christians to obey God's voice—and maybe die.

By contrast, missions for my folks and their predecessors meant blood, not dollars. "The blood of the martyrs is the seed of the church" was not a flashy aphorism for my parents and their generation of missionaries. For those who had counted the cost of breaking new ground for the kingdom, martyrdom was a real possibility.

A Family Reunion

When my father was buried in Hequ on January 1, 1940, we children were all at boarding school in Chefoo on the coast. But Mor saw to it that among all the banners from friends at the funeral, there was one from us, signed by Edvard, Kari, Hakon and Torje. The message read: "The last greeting to our dear Far [Father] with thanks for all you have meant to us," and then in large print, "IT WAS FOR JESUS' SAKE."

Forty-two years later the four of us were photographed at the site of our mother's grave in Oslo, Norway, holding this banner. It was a time to remember our magnificent heritage—the central theme of our parents' life—that there is One who is worth living and dying for. Torje, the only one of us who settled in Norway, hosted a family reunion with his wife, Reidun. Spread as we had been on four continents, we had still managed to visit each other in our travels to and fro, but this was the first time the four of us with our four spouses had been all together in one place. It became an intense time of family togetherness which added inspiration to the writing of this book. Significantly, we were reminiscing on Norwegian soil, where this story begins.

Call
to China

2

For my father, Peter Torjesen, life changed at age seventeen. It was then, at a special church meeting, that he heard Ludvig Hope, a famous Norwegian missions advocate, speak about all the places in China that had never heard of Jesus Christ.

When the sermon was over and the offering taken, it seemed to my father that there was only one thing to do. He opened his wallet and poured out all the money in it. Then he realized he had to offer more than money, and found a piece of paper and wrote the three words *Og mit liv* ("And my life"). So in an act of worship he gave the little money he had—and his life—as an offering for the kingdom to come in China.

The man who counted the collection that day was Peter's Sunday-school teacher. Immediately recognizing the handwriting, he decided to keep the note to see what would happen with this unusual promise. He had already been praying for Peter, but his prayers took on new meaning as he watched this young disciple carry out the pledge he had made to God.

Beginnings

Peter Torjesen was born on November 28, 1892 to Edvard and Elise Torjesen, known throughout their hometown of Kristiansand to be devout Christians. Edvard Torjesen had inherited the chimney-sweep director's position in town from his father, which meant ensuring that all the chimneys in town were swept regularly. Like his father before him and his son Torleif after him, my Grandfather Torjesen was expected to read Scripture and pray in each home where he came to take care of a chimney. So he was a chimney sweep who could also sweep the souls of his clients.

I remember talking to one of the old-timers in Kristiansand who said, "It was like peace came to the house when Torleif came. He would always conduct a prayer service in each home where he swept the chimney." Then she told of the newspapers placed on the floor (so the soot would not spoil the rug) from the front door to the living-room table set with white tablecloth, coffee and goodies. And of course there was a Bible, waiting for the chimney sweep to perform his major role. "Torleif could talk to people and counsel them just as his father had done before him. He always had the right word to give them," another old-timer added. Yet another told me of visiting the home where my father and his brother Torleif grew up: "There was a unique spirit about the place. It was a beautiful home." But my grandmother didn't always think it was so beautiful, as she complained about the pillowslips getting dirty so quickly. "It's as if they sweat soot!"

With lots of soot, and a houseful of boys to keep fed and clean, my grandmother could get discouraged. But then my grandfather would suggest, "Just leave the dishes and all your work. Put on your coat and walk up into the slum district." She would do that and come back with the confession "Oh, how good I have it. I have seen the drunkenness and the poverty with which others struggle. I'll never complain again."

My father referred to his Christian heritage later in his ordination sermon.

I was brought up in a godly home. We were ten children, eight brothers and two sisters. Mother gathered us around her every morning and read the Bible and prayed with us, and Father ended the day with God's Word. My parents were also missionary-minded, and I got the impression from my childhood that to be a missionary was the greatest thing anyone could want to be. From Sunday school I remember I had a relationship with God when I was eleven or twelve years old, and that the Sunday school became a time of worship for me. . . .

My brother-in-law Edvard Gerard went to China as a missionary in 1910. He soon became sick and died. But a few years before he left, he asked me to come to a prayer meeting which he and some other young men had every week. I didn't dare say no since he was the one inviting me. I knew what it would mean, that I would have to openly let the world know I was a Christian. Just then as I had finished school and started work in an office, it was a critical point in my life. . . . With a strong feeling that there was something raging inside me, I went that first night to the prayer meeting, and when all the others had prayed and waited for me to pray, all I could say was, 'God help me.' Next time I prayed I had contact with my heavenly father.

In those days there were quite a few young boys in town who were converted. They often got together in each other's homes for Bible study and prayer and also took part in various forms of outreach. Peter was among a small group of young men who started a club for younger boys in 1909, to give them a start in following Jesus. This club was under the auspices of *Ynglingen,* which was a renewal group under the umbrella of the YMCA.

By this time my father had graduated from a business college and was working for a local company as a bookkeeper, cashier, clerk and correspondent in Norwegian, English and German. He held this position for two and one-half years. Then, in 1911, Ditrik Andersen and C. T. Dyrness came from the Norwegian Evangelical Free Church in the U.S. to hold a Bible course in Kristiansand. Peter attended and the result was that when the three-week course was over, he left for America to continue his preparation for the mission field of China, to which God had called him.

But before Peter left for America, he took notice of a teen-aged girl who was as faithful as he was in going to the *bedehuset* (prayer house). They walked on opposite sides of the street on their way to these meetings, even though they lived on the same street (about one and one-half blocks apart). They were born the same year and had played together as children but, as teen-agers, serious about missions, they kept a safe distance. They were afraid of anything that might distract them from their goal of serving the Lord wholeheartedly.

I talked to people in Kristiansand who remembered my father as a young man of strong physique (a good soccer player) who after he became a serious Christian gave up playing because the games were on Sunday. The girls noticed him, but he had no time for them, some of the women complained. "His whole life even as a teen-ager was geared toward knowing God," a retired schoolmaster told me. "Of course he had his eyes on the girl down the street on Tolbodgaten, but none of us dared tease him about her."

My Mother

Living on Tolbodgaten, Valborg Tonnessen was born June 22, 1892, the daughter of a sea captain and the eldest of three children. Her father was lost at sea when his sailing ship sank in a storm. He was expected home for Christmas that year. Valborg was six at the time, and with her siblings she waited and waited, but their Pappa never came. Many years later the ship was found at the bottom of the North Sea. Going down with Pappa Tonnessen was his organ, which he played often on board, for his own enjoyment and edification, and for leading the crew in singing the great hymns of faith.

One precious letter from Pappa was kept among little Valborg's treasures:

To My Dear Daughter! Pappa is well because Jesus every day is good to me and lets me be active and healthy, and that I thank him for. Now you and Mamma must also thank him, and pray that he will get Pappa home to you again. Pappa is so glad each time I hear that you are so good to Mamma, for then I know that Mamma has it good, and that Jesus is among you there at home and his holy angels which Mamma tells you about. You must greet your teacher from Pappa and tell her that Pappa is so glad to hear that you sing about Jesus. . . .

Live well,

Your own Pappa.

Pappa had left his family a lovely brick duplex where my Mormor (mother's mother) lived all her life. This meant she always had the income from the upstairs apartment, but in those days there was no widow's pension. So to support her family Mormor bought a knitting machine and took orders for knitted garments. Little Valborg was the delivery girl, and told me how tired she would sometimes be, running for blocks with the orders. With the steps to the houses near the sidewalk, she would tell herself she only had to run to the next step, and then do the same to the next, and the next. It was her early training in the principle of taking "one step at a time."

In order to help with the family income, Mor went to work at seventeen for an import/export firm where she soon became the supervisor for the local store. At twenty she was offered a better job at the biggest department store in town. There she also rose to supervisor. When she left for China, her former boss became one of her most generous supporters. While Mor felt the sting of poverty in her childhood, she always looked back on those years as carefree and happy. Often she and her group of young Christian friends went on excursions by ski or train, usually to some convention or revival meeting. Such gatherings were characterized by happy singing and lively testimonies by those who attended.

But with her sights on the mission field, Mor knew she needed more education and entered nurse's training in 1916. As a nurse she became the favorite of a respected surgeon, who wrote on her recommendation that she was *"snar i snuen"* ("quick in her movements"). She was also his favorite anesthetist because she could tell stories to keep any patient relaxed till the anesthesia took over.

Big Decisions

Meanwhile, Far was in Rushford, Minnesota, attending a Bible school recommended by Ditrik Andersen. (The school was the forerunner of the current Trinity Evangelical Divinity School in Deerfield, Illinois.) Far writes, "There was a fresh spirit and open-heartedness there among the teachers and students which I will always remember with gratitude and joy. I stayed in Rushford three winters until in 1913 I was among the first graduating class. Then I was given opportunity to work with the free congregations, but because the mission field was my goal and I was not old enough to be a missionary yet, I continued my studies at Moody Bible Institute [MBI]."

Since the door to China was still not open, in the fall of 1916 he went on to Northern Baptist Theological Seminary in Chicago. It was there he got a telegram from his father in Norway that he was needed for military service at home, and so he discontinued his studies and went home. With World War 1 in progress, he was soon drafted: "Meet at the depot on Odderoen. November 20, 1916 at 10 a.m."

In the next two years Far got reacquainted with Valborg Tonnessen, having carried her image in his heart during the five and one-half years he had been gone. Once she returned to Kristiansand for a vacation from her nurses' training in Oslo. At vacation's end, Far saw her to the train. Suddenly, he decided to jump on the train and go with her. He had waited long enough, so it was then he proposed to her. Their friends had expected the engagement for years, and there was celebration in town. Far's brother David had always said, "If you can get Valborg you'll do well."

The marriage proposal made and his military service completed, Far applied to the Norwegian Mission in China, which had been founded when Hudson Taylor of the CIM came to Norway. Taylor's idea was that the European countries should have their own missions associated with the CIM. Now Far got better acquainted with the scattered prayer groups that were the backbone of the mission, as well as with his future bride. There were times for walking in Baneheia (the lovers lane of Kristiansand) before they faced another long separation.

Leaving for China
On his way to China in 1918, Far went via the U.S., as the Norwegian Evangelical Free Church in Brooklyn was ready to ordain him. Of course, he could have been ordained in Norway, but that would have meant additional time to meet ecclesiastical requirements there. And Far was eager to get to China.

It was that year Far chose his life verse. Upon reaching China he wrote beside Philippians 1:20:

> Motto for China, 1918: "According to my earnest expectation and my hope, that in nothing I shall be ashamed, but that with all boldness, as always, so now also Christ shall be magnified in my body, whether it be by life, or by death." (KJV)

Then he went through the prescribed two-year Chinese course of the CIM. Language school came first, followed by study with a tutor. The study of language never ceased, since there were about 60,000 monosyllabic characters (word pictures) in Chinese, and without the first 2,000 one could not even read the New Testament.

While Far was in China studying, Mor was finishing her nursing and studying a year at Indremisjonen's Bible School in Oslo. Then she went on to London for four months' training with the CIM. From there, in late 1920, she embarked on the seven-week voyage to China on a German ship together with another CIM woman missionary from Russia. Eventually she wrote home from Shanghai, "Now I am happy and well . . . a wonderful entrance to China."

Far wrote from Shanxi while Mor was on the sea:

> God helped me to visit forty villages in four to five weeks. . . . It is easier to speak with the individual . . . here than at home. . . . That callousness one finds among people at home who have resisted the light is less frequent here. I think God has heard the prayers for us. For my part I am healthy in body and happier in my soul than I have ever been before.

Language Study

Though Mor and Far were both in China, they were weeks apart. From Shanghai Mor went on to language school in Yanzhou, Jiangsu. Not until three months after her arrival did she see her fiance in Shanxi, where she was going on with her Chinese studies. Far complained to us later that there he wasn't even allowed to wink at her at the table.

That was not proper according to Chinese custom. Still Mor wrote home to her mother, "It was so good to be together. How good it would have been to be together a little longer. The four days went by much too quickly. They were wonderful and I thank God for them."

The CIM required all missionaries, men and women, to spend two years in language study before marriage. Why?

The mission was ahead of its time in accepting both husband and wife as full-fledged missionaries. Even today, many missions look on the wife as merely an encourager for the husband, not working directly in the field herself. But the CIM was practical in seeing the need for women as well as men to evangelize China. And if the wives were to be a part of this process, they too had to know the language. Yet everyone expected that once the babies were born the wife would be faced with many responsibilities at home—responsibilities that might preclude such things as language study. So Hudson Taylor made the rule that only single men and women could be accepted to the mission, and no marriages were allowed to take place in China until both husband and wife had finished two years of language study. With everyone arriving in China single, there was the added advantage of not starting off with the marrieds and the singles in separate camps.

It was a justifiable rule, but also a hard one. Waiting for Mor's two years meant Far had over four years of bachelorhood in China before their marriage on January 17, 1923. Mor arrived in China January 17, 1921, and once the two years were up, neither wanted to wait one more day!

Today a two-year waiting period sounds severe. But to my folks and their colleagues it was part of taking up the cross and bringing the gospel to China. Even during his bachelor days Far was able to write home, "I felt last fall when for the first time I was gone for a longer time—the only foreigner with my Chinese colleagues—to preach the Gospel, that instead of loneliness, there was such a wonderful peace in my soul as we traveled about."

Famine in Shanxi

In the spring of 1921, Far was asked by the Chinese government to help build roads in famine-stricken South Shanxi. The Red Cross had given a million Chinese dollars to be used for good wages for the tens of thousands of famine victims who would work on the roads and save their families from starvation. My father and two other missionaries took their turns at being the paymasters for the first road for motor vehicles in the province. But the star of the show was the future General Joseph Stillwell, whom the International Famine Relief Committee borrowed briefly from the army.

Historian Barbara Tuchman, in *Stillwell and the American Experience in China,* describes his involvement:

> Hearing of the road-building project and eager for a chance to move out and use his newly acquired Chinese under real conditions, he asked for the job. . . . The projected road link was to be 82 miles long, starting at Fenchow and finishing at Jung-tu on the Yellow River. . . . He had twelve foreign assistants including a Standard Oil civil engineer, a Swedish mining engineer, two Norwegian missionaries and an Anglo-Indian reserve officer.

That same year, Mor as a nurse was also involved with the famine victims, and wrote:

> Every day a number of sick people come. You can't imagine how wonderful it is to be able to help them. Some days we have big crowds of men, women and children from the famine districts. We may have thirty here overnight and for meals. Many are so sick and pitiful that it is hard to look at them.

Far Reaches Hequ

After his stint with the Red Cross, and having been in China three

32

years, Far was ready to open a station of his own. He asked to be sent to the hardest place, where there was no church and no one else wanted to go. There was need for someone to break new ground in the northwest corner of the province, in Hequ where the Yellow River divides Shanxi from Shaanxi to the west, and Shanxi from Inner Mongolia to the north. Far sensed a definite call to go there. And so, after five days' journey by mule, he arrived on November 5, 1921 in the city of Hequ. The name has a double meaning: either "the turn of the river" or, more poetically, "the song of the river."

Far soon discovered that a Swedish missionary had been there before him and had been killed (in south Shanxi) during the Boxer uprising. People still remembered him, but there were no visible results from his ministry.

It must have been sobering to Far to follow in the footsteps of a martyr. Hadn't Far made the same type of commitment when he chose Philippians 1:20 as his motto for China? And even earlier, when at seventeen he had promised "And my life" for China?

Enthusiastic about breaking new ground for the gospel, Far started holding meetings in his residence and accepted invitations to speak to the prisoners and the policemen. By March 12, 1922 the newly formed church in Hequ had its first baptisms: the secretary to the chief of police, the postmaster and the gatekeeper.

Later he wrote of going to Inner Mongolia.

It is a gorgeous morning. The river is bright blue with big trees along its shores. For the first time I am seeing a group of Mongols in the ferry. They are wearing necklaces and bracelets, and leather shoes. One of them is a lama going the same way . . . so we'll travel together.

But when he visited his future bride in Jinglo in 1922, she seemed more concerned with his physical welfare than these open doors. She wrote home,

33

Peter is alone in Hequ and God is with him. It was good he came here for Christmas because then he got a new cook we trained for two weeks. The one he had could only cook one thing. Morning and evening Peter got cooked rice. But now there will be some changes. I have made long lists of all the things the new cook can do. And so far Peter has had only one cup and one enamel plate. Now I have sent with him dishes and kitchen utensils.

No wonder Far used to joke about his carefree bachelor days coming to an end!

Ready for Marriage

Meanwhile, Mor was experiencing her singleness in a different way. She wrote home to Norway,

That I am thirty years old and not married the Chinese cannot imagine. Here the girls are married off as twelve- or thirteen-year-olds. So when we are visiting and a new woman comes into the room, the rest shout out, "Look at her, she is thirty and not married." One day in a very nice home four daughters-in-law watched me with a mixture of astonishment and envy. Then the oldest said, "How wonderful that you have been kept so well till now. You are thirty and not married." She thought that was great. That I was soon to get married I didn't tell them. For then the talk would have had no end.

The letter was written less than a week before Mor and Far were united in marriage in a Norwegian ceremony in Lan Xian, Shanxi. For the wedding dinner they had meatballs made from the breast of the chicken, chopped fine by hand—Chinese style—that tasted like Norwegian fishballs. The mandarin's wife sent her cook over to do the honors, giving the ceremony the official touch, as the mandarin was the national government's representative in town.

Newlyweds Pioneer in Hequ

3

The Torjesens' honeymoon was a journey to Hequ. Mor described it:
We had a good trip, not even cold or windy which we could expect
at this time of the year. God prepared everything for us in every
way. The last two days were a bit rough up and down the mountains from morning till evening. After six days we were home Sat-
urday evening and it was good to be in our own place. Our Chinese
friends had made everything so festive. The little courtyard with its
flat roofs lay smiling in the sunset, and gave such a good welcome.
And over the door of our new home the Christians had placed the
motto: "GOD'S GRACE HAS NO LIMITS."

I felt thoroughly welcome, as we ate delicious Chinese food
which they had prepared for us. Afterwards we got a few things

done before the Prayer Meeting. We hung curtains up in both rooms of our apartment, and got tablecloths on the tables.

Sunday we had meetings morning and afternoon, and for the first time the women came to church in Hequ. It seemed strange, especially for the men, who are used to being there alone. We have hung a green curtain down the middle, dividing the men from the women. Behind the curtain you can hear mumblings and loud talk from the women. If it was like this during Paul's time, it is no wonder he had to tell the women to be silent in the worship services. [1 Cor 14:34-35]

Hequ and Corinth

It is interesting Mor made the connection between the women of Hequ and those of Corinth. While theologians have argued about the meaning of the Corinthian passage for nearly 2,000 years, Mor was enlightened by an immediate object lesson in hermeneutics.

The rather obvious similarity between the two groups of women (in spite of the span of time that separated them) is women's long history of oppression and lack of education. In China, the low status of women before 1949 is hard to imagine. (And this even after the 1911 Revolution initiated changes for the better.) Traditional norms and ethics in China were codified by Confucius (551-479 B.C.) in his epigrams. He did not have one favorable word about women. In Chinese cosmology the world was divided into two elements that complemented each other: the "yin" (the female) represented everything dark and weak and passive; the "yang" (the male) represented everything strong and bright and active.

Since women were next to slaves in status, it was not socially acceptable for them to mingle with men in public. The only exception would be if a woman of unusual status, like my mother, would invite the women as her personal guests. That first Sunday must have been a day of *kairos,* or opportunity, for the women of Hequ. I can imagine my parents linking the experience with Isaiah's words "The people walking in darkness have seen a great light" (9:2). It was such a big moment in the lives of these uneducated women that they hardly knew how to behave. For they had never gone to even kindergarten or first grade, so their mothers had not initiated them with the familiar words "Now sit still and listen to the teacher, without interrupting."

For the women of Hequ, a gathering with other women was looked on as precisely a chance to talk and catch up on the news. Hence the chatter (*laleo* in the letter to the Corinthians). And later, when they began to listen intently, they would interrupt the sermon with spontaneous questions. My mother would then walk over and whisper, "Wait with that till after the service and I will talk with you, or better still, go home and discuss your question with your husband." Like Paul (1 Cor 14:35), she was encouraging dialog on spiritual issues between husband and wife—something as unheard of in patriarchal China as it had been in patriarchal Corinth.

The New Bride Makes Hequ Her Home
While Mor was catapulted into the patriarchal reality of Hequ as soon as she arrived, she did not lose touch with other practical realities. As she writes,

> The following two weeks were busy getting everything in order, both in the apartment and the station. A bachelor station is always unique. If you could have seen it, you wouldn't know whether to laugh or cry, but now it's all ready. You can't imagine what a cozy little home we've got. In the dining room we've even got a wooden floor! We also have a room for the clinic. A lot of visitors are coming to see and to hear, and are received in the men's and women's reception rooms. Most of them want to come in and see our home, so we have had full house. . . . On Sundays we have also had the church full.

One reason the bachelor station needed so much attention was Far's complete dedication to a simple lifestyle, with a willingness to give away anything that another wanted. As children we heard about the tapestry on the wall someone desired, and of course Far took it down and gave it away. No wonder his walls were as bare as his kitchen cupboards. We also heard about a beautiful white silk suit (the latest in men's fashions in those days) that Mor had used her meager allowance to buy for her beloved fiance. She told us how stunning he looked in it, with his broad shoulders and fine build. But sure enough, another missionary asked him that, living at the edge of civilization as he did, what use did he really have for a silk suit? So the precious gift was given away. Mor recounted this with a twinkle in her eye when we were young, and a little more irritation when we were adults. She admired his values, but was not sure she was called to the same austerity. And now that she was the lady of the house in Hequ, she made the best use of any local material that could make the little home cozier.

As soon as the home base was in order, Far was eager to show Mor around the city that he had written home about so enthusiastically. He had described Hequ "as part of a flat prairie with meadows to the East and the Yellow River winding its way through the West of town like the Torridals River in Kristiansand. The population is also about 10,000 to 15,000, the same as Kristiansand, with about 100,000 in the county of Hequ. And if you have plenty of time let's take a walk on the Great Wall of China which has one arm reaching Hequ." Built between 246 and 209 B.C. and 1,500 miles long, the Great Wall defined the historical boundary between China and Mongolia.

Telling the Story to Those Who Had Never Heard

Soon the newlyweds settled into a routine of gospel proclamation, taking care of the sick, and later starting an elementary school for the children—the first school in Hequ's history to admit girls.

For Mor telling the story of God's love meant visiting in the homes of the women. For Far it meant sharing the story with the men in the market. When he later tried to rent space for a street chapel in the business district (so the gospel story could be told with less interruption from the market), he found that people were too superstitious to rent to the "foreign devils." They preferred to rent to Chinese for half the price.

Among the women who came to see Mor there was superstition. Everyone who came was offered a cup of tea, according to good Chinese custom, but Mor writes,

Most women are afraid to drink tea here in the women's reception room, even though it is Chinese tea, bought here in town. They think we put a kind of medicine in the tea to bewitch them to turn to our teaching about God. The men on the other hand who have had contact with us longer, have more confidence in us and are not afraid to drink our tea.

Seeing Other Missionaries after Six Months
With all the new adjustments, and having spent almost six months without seeing any other foreigners, the summer vacation at Sommerly came as a welcome change—even if it meant five days on the back of a mule to get there. Sommerly was the Norwegian name given to a deserted place up in the mountains. It was surrounded by pine trees and rocks, and a stream ran through it. Each family built its own tiny flat-roofed, mud-brick hut to get away from the summer heat and epidemics of the plains, and to have a chance to meet with their scattered fellow-workers from the same mission.

For Mor and Far the vacation at Sommerly that year meant a second chance for a wedding reception. Because transportation was by mule, only three of the missionaries had made it to the wedding. Another factor was that the goodies sent from Norway months in

39

advance had arrived too late for the big day, but not too late for Sommerly. Mor writes to her mother about the feast:

We invited everyone to the pine forest just above our hut. You can imagine the surprise when we opened the lids to find real Norwegian fishballs in white sauce, served with steaming hot potatoes. And then we had the "kransekake" (the traditional wedding cake made from ground almonds), the princess cake, and the chocolate you sent. Everyone praised you for having sent such good things and send their greetings and thanks. You can't imagine the excitement.

The Opium Crime

Refreshed by the time away, Mor and Far returned to Hequ with new vigor for their overwhelming task. Often in their writings they mention the 100,000 people in the county, among whom only a handful were believers. They tell of the immorality and opium addiction that ruined homes. While opium was outlawed in Shanxi, across the river in Inner Mongolia, laws against opium were not enforced. So many from Hequ went north looking for jobs and returned home ruined.

In one of her letters, Mor writes with great concern about a twelve-year-old girl who had been sold by her father to an opium smoker, to become his bride when she turned sixteen. But the future groom was so angry with her father's interest in the gospel that he almost killed him on a lonely road.

Opium is one of the greatest curses brought by the West to China. "It despoiled great areas of land, ruined millions of homes . . . and eventually led to war in 1840," wrote Carrington Goodrich. In 1729, the sale of opium had been forbidden by imperial decree, and in 1800 the importation of the drug was forbidden. "In spite of this ban," continues Goodrich, "5,000 chests annually were entering Canton by 1821, most of it on British vessels but part of it on American and other ships."

When the Chinese government burned a huge consignment, war with Britain resulted. But just prior to this, a Chinese official who had arrested many opium dealers appealed to Queen Victoria:

There appear among the crowd of barbarians both good persons and bad. Consequently, there are those who smuggle opium to seduce the Chinese people. . . . Let us ask, where is their conscience? I have heard that the smoking of opium is very strictly forbidden by your country. . . . Suppose there were people from another country who carried opium for sale to England and seduced your people into buying and smoking it. . . . May you, O Queen, check your wicked and sift your vicious people before they come to China.

Finally in 1911 the Parliament forbade the shipment of opium to China. By the time my parents reached Hequ, the capital city of Yunnan in the south had 90 per cent of the men and 60 per cent of the women addicted to opium smoking. Fortunately, it was not as bad as that in Hequ or in Inner Mongolia. But my parents bore the disgrace of knowing where the opium had come from. Around the middle of the nineteenth century the same nations that wanted opium legalized, asked for tolerance for missionary activity.

Foot-Binding

But not all evils could be blamed on the West. From her first arrival in Hequ, Mor continued to battle against the second-class status of women. The foot-binding of women was but one illustration of their oppression through the centuries. While the feet of new baby girls were no longer bound in Hequ, most of the grown women had bound feet.

The binding of women's feet dates back to the tenth century. A foot reduced to three inches from heel to toe was seen as a mark of gentility—the perfect beautiful foot, called the Golden Lily. But with all the efforts to romanticize the custom, the real purpose of the barbarous custom was voiced in the Chinese proverb "Feet are bound, not to make them beautiful as a curved bow, but to restrain women when they go out of doors."

Men and women lived in two worlds, the public and the private. To be sure a woman would never forget where she belonged, her foot was permanently crippled. She could never leave the house without feeling the pain of her bound feet.

The binding process, which started in a little girl's first or second year, was excruciatingly painful. I remember sitting around the *kang* (the heated brick platform used for sitting and sleeping) and hearing the tales of the recent past when screams and tantrums had accompanied the cruel process. Initially just cloth bandages were used, but later wire was used to be sure the foot would not return to normal. At some point, when the crippling was complete, the wire was removed.

Once I asked one of the women I loved dearly to show me her foot. After removing her cloth shoes, she slowly unwound the bandages that gave her foot some form and security. All that was left was a stub. The sight revolted me and filled me with pity for this woman. It also caused me to marvel how these women could walk about and accomplish all they did, when every step had to be painful. And to think of all the women who walked with Mor—taking the good news from house to house with bound feet!

These women were called "Bible women" because they always carried Bibles, and they were among the few women in town who could read. Usually when they had made contact in a home they would offer to read from the Book. Later the term "Bible women" was also used for those who worked full-time for the church in women's work.

The Joy of Starting a Family

In the middle of all the adjustments to a new culture, God gave Mor and Far the joy of their hearts in their first child, Edvard. Born on February 17, 1924, he was named after his Grandpa Torjesen. Beginning then the letters home centered on the new member of the family. Edvard came to fill a deep need in their life in the loneliness of a new outpost. "Many men and women come to see our little Edvard," Mor writes later. "He laughs and jabbers to everyone, so we have rich opportunities to witness about our Savior Jesus Christ."

Before Edvard was two years old, Mor was counting on him as a missionary partner. She writes home,

> Three mornings a week I teach the little girls who come here to learn how to read, and three days I visit women in their homes. Edvard comes along and he likes that. I don't have a Bible woman to go with me now, so he is my companion. It is not proper for me as a woman to go out in the city alone, but it's all right with my son as my escort. In this way he takes the place of the Bible woman. It's beginning early, isn't it?

The Family Enjoys a Vacation

I was born at Sommerly, August 8, 1925, and named after my Mormor (mother's mother) Karoline, which was cut short to Kari. It rained that day and the mud-roof leaked, I was told. And wherever the little basket with me in it was moved, the leaking would start. But letters home referred to me as "solstralen" (ray of sunlight), so it couldn't have damaged my disposition too much.

Sverre Holth, a valued colleague, had just arrived from Norway and stayed with us in our little hut called "Solbakken" that summer. He was still full of stories about it when I last visited him at the church he pastors in Oslo: "Oh, Valborg was good at making everything festive at Sommerly. She would get us together for meals and coffees and music evenings where we all played our instruments. She was the life of the party. It's typical of people from Kristiansand to be good at entertaining." He continued:

You know both Peter and Valborg had strong convictions—not always the same as others. It could lead to conflicts, but I never had any conflict with them. I enjoyed the bull sessions. It was fun to discuss back and forth. Peter thought I was too liberal. He loved to argue with someone who differed with him. That was like a sport for him, discussing theology. And then he was so full of stories and he would laugh so heartily as he told them, stories about different characters in Kristiansand. I'd hear them many times. He was lots of fun. Strong convictions, but never of a gloomy disposition.

He went on about their marriage.

Valborg was the strong one who added color to everything. Peter would always say, "Valborg, you decide." Of course he was involved in all big decisions, but most of life is little ones. I never saw any friction between them. It was a harmonious relationship. They were happy. But the secret was their loyalty to each other. And they were festive people to be around.

Every summer we were back at Sommerly with people like Onkel Sverre who later got married and built his own hut on the hill. When I got older I realized that Sommerly was not only for vacation. Since it was the only place the missionaries were all together, areas of cooperation in the work were decided here, and reports from each station shared. For the year 1925 Mor and Far's report included: Four men had been baptized, they had special meetings twice with people from the outside coming, Far had worked at two out-stations, 367 street meetings had been held, 242 villages had been visited, and about 22,000 people had heard the gospel. Of Bible portions and small books 2,000 had been sold, and 16,000 tracts distributed. Many sick had been treated and medicines given out. Numerous homes had been visited. And Sunday mornings there were about twenty at the worship service.

The next year, it was decided that after Sommerly Mor and we two kids would go to Lin Xian and stay with the missionaries there for the fall. Far, meanwhile, would return to Hequ alone to try to do something about the disrepair of our house. It still had not been possible to either rent or buy anything better, but they badly needed larger facilities so that, according to Chinese custom, there could be separate courtyards for men and women. The 1925 annual report also said that for lack of space the school they had started had been closed. But some of the little girls continued their schooling informally with Mor, as there were no other schools available for girls.

Far Down with Typhoid Fever

After two months alone in Hequ, Far was on his way to Lin Xian for Christmas, but didn't make it further than Shuo Xian before he came down with typhoid fever. Some good Swedish missionaries took him in and wired Mor. She writes home, "We had some critical days—a life or death struggle, but the eighteenth day the fever broke. God stepped in with his mighty hand. It is now the twenty-eighth day and the last few days there has been no fever." She continued:

> Peter was so happy under the whole illness and seemed to live in the "heavenlies" so it was a blessing for all of us who stood around him. Even in his feverish hallucinations he thought God still had a job for him to do in China, and that his life would be spared for my sake and the children's. When I think of all the missionaries who have died of typhoid in Shanxi and the next province, and that all over China it is the cause of most deaths in the CIM, then I realize that it is only God's mercy that Peter's life has been spared.

Soon after we were all reunited back in Hequ, another crisis—a political one—broke out all over China. By the spring of 1927 there was a clash of ideology and leadership between the Reds and the Kuomintang (National People's Party), with many ramifications. Warlords in different provinces were looking out for their own interests, and foreigners in general were blamed, rightly and wrongly, for the problems of China. Hence most missionaries were forced to leave their posts. Five thousand missionaries were evacuated, some never to return.

Furlough in Norway

Since it was Far's ninth year in China and Mor's seventh, we were granted a furlough in Norway in 1927. Mormor took us in at Tolbodgaten in Kristiansand, and we had a great reunion with the family on both sides. Each time I go home the stories grow of Edvard's and my behavior that year. Just as in China we took on missionary work early, in Norway Mor sent us to the store down the street to buy milk when Edvard was three and I was two! We would have the order written on a slip of paper wrapped around the coins that would pay for it. On the way we stopped on the steps of houses and played with the coins. It was fun seeing them roll down to the gutter near the sidewalk. But by the time we reached the store there weren't enough coins left to pay the bill.

There were also stories about me following Edvard everywhere he went. He couldn't even go to the bathroom without me saying, "Kari *ogsa"* ("also"). But in those good old days of outhouses with two or three holes, this was not the invasion of privacy it would be today.

During furlough Hakon was born (May 9, 1928) and named after Captain Hakon Tonnessen, the grandfather lost at sea in whose house we were staying. Once more there were the cries and laughter of three little ones in that house—just as there had been once before when Mormor was first widowed. How she loved having us with her that year. But we weren't there for long. Soon the house was bustling with activity as the shopping and packing started. Clothes and supplies— enough to last five people for seven years—were tucked into the wooden trunks Far had built. Hakon was four months old and ready to travel.

The Journey Is Our Home

And so we started the seven-and-one-half week journey back to Hequ. First we traveled by ship to Oslo, then by train for two weeks— through Sweden, across the waters to Germany and Poland, and on through Russia and Siberia to China. Imagine Mor with three lively youngsters. And as Far was buying food on one station, the train took off. But he managed to hop on the last car and finally after a long walk through the train cars, reached a rather apprehensive family who welcomed him as a returned hero. The train journey ended at Dalian, where we waited ten days for a ship to Tianjin. Then we went by train to Taiyuan, where we had to wait six days for mules. They took us the last ten days home to Hequ.

In spite of weariness after travel, Mor and Far were thrilled to be back. When they reached Hequ, missionary Georg Rinvold was waiting for them since he had been in Hequ during their absence. It was Georg who wrote in the mission paper, "When the China Inland Mission around the turn of the century gave us as a mission this impassable mountainous district, it was with the comment that only Norwegians were rugged enough to take it."

On the long journey, the last ten days had been the hardest and the happiest. I can see Far walking as much as he was riding the slow mule, a stubborn animal that seemed bent on applying the psalm: "I have set the LORD always before me; Because He is at my right hand I shall not be moved" (16:8 NKJV). Yet there was something peaceful about the slow rhythm of the mules, and the fact that we could get off and walk ahead on the road and wait for the mules to catch up.

Almost without realizing it, these long journeys began to seem like home to us. They strengthened our identity as a pilgrim family who easily saw our own experiences in the images of the great hymn "Lead On O King Eternal":

Lead on, o' fiery pillar,

We follow without fears,
But we shall come rejoicing
Though joy be born of tears;
We are not lost though wandering,
For by your light we come,
And we are still God's people,
The journey is our home!

The Song
of the River
Calls Us Home

4

In 1928 the civil war was over. All over China missionaries were returning to their posts. The Song of the River (the meaning of the name Hequ) had also lured us back. It had merged with another song, in our native Norwegian language, *"Ut a fiske for din mester"* ("Go Out and Fish for Your Master"). However, the songs harmonized more in the hearts of my parents than in outward circumstances. Three problems continued to plague the country. First, tension was developing between Chiang Kai-shek's Kuomintang (Nationalist People's Party) and the newly formed Communists' "Red Army." Second, hundreds of thousands of soldiers had been recruited during the civil war and were now roaming the country as a threat to peace and order. And third, banditry had become a way of life for thousands of disillusioned men who weren't soldiers.

Edvard remembers meeting some of the bandits as we traveled by mule over the sandy hills of Shanxi. When Far saw the robbers he crossed over to the other side of the ravine to negotiate with them, while the rest of the family prayed. Far returned barefooted. The bandit chief had wanted his shoes, but miraculously had sent Far back to us safe.

Another time, at Sommerly, we heard the bandits were coming and all the grownups gathered for prayer. Then we children, about ten of us, decided we should also pray. I remember the certainty I had that God had heard us. When the adults finished praying, they couldn't find the children and panicked. Had the robbers taken us while they were praying? Then they found us in one of the houses, all on our knees. With faith strengthened but still doubting, everyone scanned the horizon for movements. Eventually word reached us from the village below that the bandits had fled. Some of the bandits had told the villagers that they had seen on our roofs men dressed in white with shining swords in their hands. They asked, "Where do they keep their army?" So at age five I knew that "the angel of the LORD encamps around those who fear him, and he delivers them" (Ps 34:7).

We learned early in life that the world had plenty of evil in it, but in our home there was tremendous security. The enemy was without, not within. At home there were love and hugs, as well as strict discipline. "Your will is in my back pocket," Far used to say, laughingly. He wasn't mean about it. It was just a fact. We knew our boundaries and we knew we were loved. And so home became the safest place in the world.

One of the pictures of home I have carried with me through life is Mor sitting on Far's lap. He'd have kept her there for hours, but she usually had to get up and attend to some duty. And then we kids would all fight for the seat of honor. It felt very safe to sit there. And in the morning it felt good to get into bed with Mor for a good snuggle-time before the day began. We fought for the space next to her and when I got there, Hakon would always sneak in between me and her. By the time we got to Mor's bed, Far had already been up since 5 a.m. for his time alone with God. Later Edvard followed his example.

The Family at Prayer

But Far did more than pray in secret. He also prayed before us. I can still see him walking the length of our living room with his eyes half-closed. We could play around him and talk to each other, but not to him, for he was talking to God. Then he would get his Bible and sit in an easy chair and read and read as if it were the most exciting novel in the world. He studied in his office with pen and paper and commentaries, but when he read Scripture he did it in front of us. Mor did the same. I can see her praying with her head buried in the chair where she was kneeling. We could also play around her, even climb on her back and take off her shoes. But we could not talk to her—she was talking to Jesus. My folks thought Jesus' counsel to pray in secret meant not making a display of it outside the home. But they felt perfectly free to pray before us, thus modeling prayer at home.

In addition to private devotions, we had prayers as a family three times a day. After breakfast we had Bible reading with everyone who could read taking part. This was followed by prayer. At night it was bedtime Bible story and each of us praying individually. And at noon we prayed through the list of 1,300 CIM missionaries, dividing them among the days of the week. This ritual led to the invention of the "Mr. and Mrs. Game." With many nationalities on the list there were some funny-sounding names.

During long trips by mule we made up even funnier names for "Mr. and Mrs.," with laughter for each. Remembering the name "Hayman,"

Hakon would shout out, "Mr. and Mrs. Hei mann tralalala," and I would come back with, "Mr. and Mrs. Kappuchet-chit-chat." We also liked to Norwegianize names—"Mr. and Mrs. Vippleson" for Whipple. All this to forget the slow mule.

The Family at Work and Play

With Mor's and Far's vision of building a family for God, as well as a church, they physically separated the ministry from the home. After furlough, a separate church property was acquired and repaired. Far wrote home: "Now we go to church like other proper people and meet church-goers on the way. Before everyone just came to us."

Next, the old dilapidated place Far had moved into in 1921 was renovated. During this time Mor and Hakon, with four women who had never ridden before or been out of town, spent four days on mules to get to a two-week women's conference. With their bound little feet these women couldn't just get off the mule and walk when the hill was steep, but they bravely rode on. A dynamic preacher from Denmark was used of God to meet these women's deep spiritual needs, which made it all worthwhile.

Meanwhile, back home Edvard and I were having fun with Far, who would joke about not being able to find our clothes, though every cupboard was left in the neatest order by Mor. Far was laid-back and let us get as dirty as we liked among all the novel building materials in the yard.

When Mor returned with the women, all full of stories about the first conference experience, Ragnhild Syvertsen came with them to join in the women's work in Hequ. Martin Jensen had already come to assist in the men's work. Both these colleagues had been at the wedding and Mor and Far were delighted to have them join the team. It was Tante Ragnhild who later told of Far's favorite attention-getting device when preaching in the market. People would be busy buying and selling and might listen for a moment and then get back to business. Then Far would suddenly say, "Do you know that I am one of eight brothers at home and we are all alive today?" Immediately he had everyone's ear. In a patriarchal culture many sons was a sign of good luck, and with the high infant mortality, few had ever heard of eight sons living to manhood. So the Christians were often asked by the townspeople, "Where's the man who is one of eight brothers?"

When missionary Thora Johansen arrived in Hequ a year later, Far had his match in practical jokes. They had a way of egging each other on. Once she dared him to get up in the pulpit the next Sunday morning with only half his face shaven. And he did! It was the foreigners who had the hard time remaining composed through the sermon, with that clown behind the pulpit. Far really wasn't too worried about what the locals thought of his pranks: "We are so strange to them anyway, in so many of our customs, that one more aberration won't make that much difference."

Far's ability to joke and tell stories kept us going in Hequ and amused his colleagues at Sommerly. "You could tell by looking at him that he was brewing a story," one told me.

We would watch him rub his knees and start laughing. "Now you'd better come with it," we would tell him. Then would come a story about the missionary who spoke about getting ready for the Second Coming. One man responded, "Oh, good, then I'll get to inherit the pastor's cow when he goes up."

Then there was the time Peter came to the Xing Xian board meeting and arriving hungry from a full day's travel by mule, coffee and open-faced sandwiches were set before him. But he didn't see the food. He just started rubbing his knees and telling stories. Later when dinner was served he said, "Oh, now it's good to get some food." Though hungry, he had been too distracted to notice the food earlier.

Besides stories about missionaries who used a wrong Chinese tone in a sermon and lost their audience, Far would pick up stories in his work in Hequ. He was proud of Mor's work in the clinic, work which she continued daily as a way of showing people that Christians cared not only in word but in deed. Mor's clinic was the only place in town where modern medicine was practiced. But suddenly she got competition. A man went to the provincial capital, bought some medicines and returned to Hequ to go into the medicine business. He had someone teach him how to write "I AM A DOCTOR" in English. But when he returned to Hequ to put up his shingle, he got the words mixed up and wrote, "AM I A DOCTOR." For years that was the only sign in English in Hequ.

Sometimes Far would tell stories of meeting a Chinese Christian who called himself an Irish Presbyterian, or good Chinese brothers and sisters who called themselves German Lutherans or Swedish Pentecostals. We were all capable of getting our nationality mixed up with our Christian persuasion, but at least Far joked about it. He could also startle his children and colleagues by asking, "What would you rather be? Dumber than you look? Or look dumber than you are?" As we struggled with the implications of such a dilemma Far would roar with laughter, especially if we took it too seriously.

Famine Followed by Severe Cold

The ability to laugh at circumstances and themselves was a key to Mor's and Far's survival in a part of the world where there was much pain. Edgar Snow, an authority on China, estimates that between five to ten million people died in the Great Famine in northwest China from 1929 to 1931. While 1929 was a year of famine, the winter of 1930 included famine and such severe cold that prisoners froze to death in the Hequ jail. Earlier people had stayed alive on leaves and the bark of trees. But with the cold, even this could not help and untold thousands died. In a patriarchal society women were the first to suffer when starvation was imminent. Hence women were sold into slavery, to be resold as wives or concubines in other parts of China. Mor writes,

It is so sad here in Hequ to see people selling their wives. Last year it was the famine that drove them to it, but things are still not normal and people can't manage to eat. The saddest is to see homes broken. Motherless children cry for mother, unhappy mothers cry for their children, and the husband may begin to smoke opium to dull the pain, and end up as a beggar. In a home nearby the wife has been sold. We tried to help them last year and this year, but when everything had been eaten, the need was just as great.

First to be sold was the five-year-old girl, and the husband threatened that the wife would be next. Her weeping and begging to stay didn't help. Then the day came when she had to leave. It took a few days as what was important was to find the buyer who would give the most money for her. The buyers usually come from the South. She was fortunate to be allowed to bring her youngest boy with her. But since then we have heard that the husband only weeps and has quit working. The ten-year-old boy who is home is also mourning, and the sixteen-year-old daughter who is married looks devastated. The mother is sold. Sent off as a slave. No more home. Everything looks dark for them. Without hope and without God to go to in their sorrow.

I grew up with a strong sense of contrast between the homes of Christains in Hequ and the homes of those who did not know God and had nowhere to go with their problems. We always had such a sense of the overwhelming goodness of God to us for food to eat and healthy bodies and a secure home. Into this setting came people from the worst famine-stricken areas, with bloated stomachs and sad faces. They sat around the yard as a warm meal was prepared for them.

This time was also my early introduction to discrimination against women. Why did the mothers and daughters have to be sold so the rest of the family could eat? While Mor understood how, when the whole family was starving, it was tempting to sell one member and have money for food, she also attributed all such practices to pagan values. "All discrimination against women has pagan roots," she told me. Female infanticide was common among the poor, as girls were an expense to raise, would need a dowry to marry and then spend their most productive years with the husband's family. I shall never forget a walk in a ravine, where we found the body of a female baby, covered with flies.

The Joys and Pains of Missionary Children
So our life in China was one of mixed suffering and joy. A joyful event occurred on October 29, 1931, when Torje was born. When Far first held his fourth child, he dedicated him to the Lord and then said, "This boy will be the joy of my old age." But before Torje had a chance to distinguish himself as someone other than an infant who ate and slept, and cooed and smiled, Edvard left for Norway in March 1932. It was like the changing of the guards. Suddenly I discovered the joy of a baby brother, along with the pain of losing an older one.

The education of us children had been a subject of much prayer for years. When Edvard was ready for grade one, Mor started teaching him the Norwegian curriculum at home. But Mor and Far felt there was more to school than the "three R's." The mission eventually sent a teacher to a school in Lin Xian, eight days' journey by mule from Hequ. If we had been sent there, we could only have seen our folks in the summer. Getting home would have meant Far fetching us and bringing us back, adding up to thirty-two days of travel by mule.

So, with these and other considerations, our parents decided to send Edvard home to Norway. Mor wrote home to her mother a month before Edvard left:

After having sought God's guidance, it still looks as if it is God's will that our dear little Edvard should go home to Norway for his schooling. We have been weighing the question for some time and God seems to have opened the way for him. Edvard himself has for a long time been praying to God to show him where he should go to school, and we thank God daily that he showed him and answered his prayer.

So at eight years old, Edvard was sent to Norway with one of the missionary families going on furlough. In Kristiansand Edvard was received into the home of Mor's brother and his wife. They had no children, but had taken in two other nephews whose parents were missionaries in Madagascar. Now three missionary nephews became their family. It was a good home, but at school Edvard was called *kineseren* ("chink"), for the same reasons he had been called "foreign devil" in Hequ. He had moved from one set of cultural adjustments to another and now had no parents to help him. Meanwhile Mor wrote from China, "We thank God for opening a good home for Edvard in Norway, but here the separation cannot be forgotten a single day by his mother and father."

I was only six, but I can still remember the pain. My first thought in the morning when I woke was, "Edvard is gone," and then of the games I couldn't play with him. For me life seemed boring and empty without the one I had been with all my short life.

For my parents, this was undoubtedly one of the most difficult decisions in their missionary career, but one in which they had to rest in the confidence that they had been led of the Lord. Yet they were also children of their time and its customs. We all conform to the Christian values of our peers. None of us, however sincere we are in following the Lord, can be sure that we are always hearing God's voice rather than merely the voices of surrounding Christians. For our folks, it seemed more important educationally and socially for Edvard to be in school with others his age, and in a Christian culture, than to be with his parents.

Years later, when Edvard was back in China, the subject of sending him to Norway came up unexpectedly. A group of missionary children at the Chefoo School were baptized in the ocean. It was a moving ceremony. Then suddenly Edvard blurted out, "But they didn't bless the water."

As Far looked at Mor and said, "You see, we shouldn't have sent him to Norway," Edvard pricked up his ears. Far knew it was during Edvard's four years of only Lutheran Christian training, in contrast to the more ecumenical teaching of the CIM, that Edvard had learned that baptismal water should be blessed. But it wasn't the detail about the water that captivated Edvard. What interested him was what lay behind the remark. Perhaps all along Far had questioned sending Edvard to Norway at age eight.

At any rate, while Edvard was away practical Mor wisely gave me a lot of responsibility in caring for little Torje. This helped get my mind off the loss of Edvard during his four years away. As Torje grew, and Hakon and I got closer, there was a tremendous bonding between us. Years later, in high school, Torje wrote of these years,

I remember my childhood home in North China by the Great Wall . . . made of mud brick with straw. In the inside courtyard we had lots of beautiful flowers. . . . In the outer courtyard we grew tomatoes. . . . Here we also kept five or six goats and chickens. We were never short of milk, and Mor made good butter and cream. I remember my big sister Kari always having great concern about me. When I was ready for a spanking she felt sorry for me. Sometimes she would even offer to be spanked for me. Other times when we had received candy from Norway, she would save her part, and when I was crying and needed comfort she would give me some. I also remember the Chinese woman who helped take care of us.

She was always good to us and told us exciting fairy tales. . . .
Another memory is gathering my Chinese playmates and telling
them about Jesus. . . . My memories of childhood are few, but very
good.

I have similarly rich memories. No tomato anywhere has since
matched the taste of a Hequ one. And I fondly remember the smell
of the goats that produced such rich milk. But my taste for that milk
got me into trouble when we stopped at some good Swedes' house
overnight on our way to the Chinese coast. "They put water in the
milk," I whispered to Mor at the breakfast table. My first taste of
cow's milk since Norway, at age three, resulted in a reprimanding look
from Mor as she apologized to our hosts.

We were on our way to the coast to spend our first summer at
Beidaihe. Far wrote to Edvard about the trip, "If only you could come
with us. We miss you so much, especially when we are planning something that will be such fun. Then we wish so much you could be here."
There were two attractions at Beidaihe—the ocean to swim in and Dr.
Donald Barnhouse, who was speaking at the Beidaihe Conference that
summer. Years later I awed the great Bible teacher by telling him of
our trip to hear him in 1934: eight twelve-hour days on mules, one day
by cart, one by bus, and over twenty-four hours by train.

Of course when we got there and started swimming twice a day it
was more than worth the effort. But when the summer was over we
had had so much fun with the other missionary children that we
wondered why our parents couldn't just tell people about Jesus in
Beidaihe. The reaction was natural and didn't worry Far and Mor.
Once back in Hequ, we settled into the old routine with the warmth
and security that our own home environment provided.

Mor writes home to Mormor, "Hakon is the same quiet fun-loving
boy, always content. Even if there isn't too much around him to stim-
ulate him, he has his own world of fantasy and dreams. . . . It's fun

to see the difference in them. Torje is so much like Edvard. But Hakon reminds me of Pappa, yes, he will be a Kvarnes boy [where Pappa came from]." Again to Mormor she writes,

Hakon is now imagining that he is so lonesome for Mormor and she for him. "I am born at Mormor's, and therefore she is so fond of me and lonesome for me." . . . Yesterday, he came suddenly running in from play and said, "I am tired of being in this country— can't we go to Norway?" We can't understand where he gets all these ideas, but he does have a lively imagination. [It is] also when he prays. Yes, he prays so even the serious-minded [fellow mission- ary] Jensen has to smile in the middle of the prayer.

Harmony at Home

Like our folks, we were living in many different worlds. In Hequ there was the world of our secure home, and the world beyond with over 100,000 people in the county who needed to hear the gospel. But while we lived in more than one world, there was harmony between our worlds. This came from the overarching unity of having a single focus as a family. We were in Hequ to show by life and by proclamation how Christ can transform human beings.

Because Mor and Far were both called to preach, there was a col- legiality between them that a traditional pastor and pastor's wife, each with their distinctive roles, do not have. Mor and Far had an egali- tarian marriage, in which there was no "captain of the ship" to call the shots. Instead, decision-making, preaching and the care of the children (including home schooling) was all a joint venture for hus- band and wife.

Chinese custom necessitated that men be evangelized by men and women by women. This meant that Far and Mor would each, at times, be away from the house. But they were conscientious about our phys- ical and spiritual safety. They did not leave us alone with our Chinese playmates, or local adult visitors, who might indoctrinate us with pagan superstitions. Their rule was that one of them was always at home. This was also good for their work, as anyone who had walked for miles or days to see them could count on finding one of them.

But this arrangement took careful planning. Mor purposely had the clinic and some of the women's Bible studies in our home. But when she went out to visit from house to house in pagan homes, or to teach Bible classes in the homes of interested women, Far was on duty at home. Of course when he traveled to villages and was gone for a week or more, Mor had to limit her local outreach.

In the Hequ church Mor and two single missionary women took their turns at preaching. And soon there were also Chinese men who were trained to preach. (To train local women at his point would have demanded too much of a cultural jump.) Usually Mor's preaching was more dramatic than Far's, with lots of stories from the Bible and daily life. Far's preaching was more centered in the story of the cross and the application of taking up the cross personally. This he seasoned with illustrations from Chinese culture. His sermons were heard in the church and the market and on the road as he met people who asked him about his teaching. He wouldn't ride a bicycle as most people walked in those days, and he hated to think of passing someone who might have a question.

But sometimes he would get discouraged. After a long answer to a question, the men who asked might draw the conversation to a polite close with, "Thank you! That's a beautiful story." On another occasion, he really thought his listener was getting closer to Jesus, as the man moved closer and closer to Far. But when Far finally asked him, "Do you have any more questions?" he replied, "How much do those sunglasses of yours cost?"

On his journeys to villages around Hequ, Far also tells of the oppression he felt among those who worshiped idols and lived in fear of evil spirits. The only way to overcome the oppressive atmosphere around him, Far said, was to "recite Bible verses, sing hymns about the cross and keep close to God in prayer."

I recall Far coming home from winter missionary journeys with a terrible cold. At such times he would reject Mor's nursing skills for a Chinese concoction of hot peppers, ginger and garlic in plenty of boiling water. Next, instead of going to bed, he would go for a long walk to sweat it off. "If you lie down, the cold gets more entrenched in you," he would tell us. If the runny nose persisted after the walk, Far would get a sheet to blow it with to dramatize the fact that his hankies were too small for such a huge cold. All this with a twinkle in his eyes, to amuse us kids.

While our life was secure in the rhythm of Mor's and Far's work and the regularity of our home life, there were few breaks from the routine—except summer vacations. We didn't live on the way to anywhere, so no missionaries would come through Hequ. But one day a German engineer surprised us. He had been hired by the government to study the possibility of a road system in Shanxi. As long as he stayed in Hequ, Mor sent him a warm European dinner every day, and of course we entertained him in our home. He was fond of music and saw the little organ that had made its way to Hequ by mule, so he asked Mor to play for him. She first played one of her favorites, Handel's "Largo," and then continued with Edvard Grieg, singing "Solveig's Song" as she played. That's when the brave engineer broke into tears. He could hardly believe that he could hear such heavenly music so far away from home, and in such a remote place as Hequ. But Mor and Far were as moved as the German was. He came to them like an angel sent by God, just when they needed the break most.

Revival Comes to Hequ
Refreshed, Mor and Far went back to their work, which during their

last years before furlough was the most encouraging to date. Constantly people were convicted of sin, repented and found their peace with God. In addition to the preaching that was done in the open market, in the surrounding villages and in the homes, there were special church meetings every year. Far writes about one series of revival meetings with an evangelist named Chang:

In the past we have emphasized Jesus' work of redemption and invited people to come to faith in Christ. But many who came never saw themselves as sinners. We are therefore thankful for Chang's ministry among us. His main theme for ten days was sin. Many of the Christians too confessed sin, that they had never before seen as sin. It gave them a new vision of grace. We are grateful for God's reviving spirit among us. We hope now it will be easier for the shepherds to lead the believers into a greater joy because of the treasures they own in Jesus Christ.

Then came the fall of 1934, when God visited Hequ in a special way. It seemed like the breakthrough Mor and Far had prayed for over the years had at last come to pass. Jean Graham of the CIM from New Zealand, who was in demand for meetings all over China, was the preacher. Mor wrote about the revival, first to Edvard:

It was two in the afternoon when I got home from the morning meeting. The Holy Spirit is working in the congregation and when the invitation was given for all who wanted to get rid of their sin, nearly all the women who had not made a stand before came forward. Others came too[,] who had some sin hindering their walk with God—altogether fifteen to twenty women. Some were crushed under the burden of sin and wept with despair. It's a time I will never forget. Our hearts were filled with thanks that we could experience something like this . . . in Hequ. A number of the women got rid of their burdens and left the church with joy on their faces. Many people have joined us these days, and among them quite a few men. The Holy Spirit is also working among the boys, including Djijon and Mansjeentsi, your friends from Sunday School. One boy whose parents are not believers went home last night and said he had become a Christian. He was among the first to come today. Oh, that this might be a great overturning for Hequ and many will be set free.

Far also wrote home to Norway, "It is amazing how God has used Miss Graham from New Zealand to bring revival among us. She has a sound view on the fullness of the Holy Spirit, and is a great encouragement to the missionaries wherever she goes." I remember those meetings as one of the greatest spiritual highlights of my life, and had my own encounter with God as a nine-year-old. As children we caught the spirit of joy that was so evident in the revival. Later Mor and Far wrote two articles home about it:

Imagine experiencing the Holy Spirit reviving the whole church, like an old-fashioned Norwegian revival with aftermeetings and tears, and confession of sin. How we've been of little faith thinking this could not happen here. We have seen conviction of sin among a few before, but to see the whole congregation gripped by the Holy Spirit was something new. . . . One woman sat there so burdened when I approached her. "I am such a big sinner that there is not one of the ten commandments I have not broken," she confessed. After pouring out her heart in prayer she arose with a smile through her tears. Beside her sat her daughter. When she saw her mother under such conviction, she broke down too.

Mor goes on to describe how this girl joined a friend in prayer, "[A]nd oh, what a confession of sin, even among these children." When the friend got home and told her story, her brother began to cry. He also gave his heart to Jesus and came to the meetings. She also describes

a man who has been a Christian several years who became so convicted of sin by the Holy Spirit that we had to pray for him more than once. Only when he promised God he would pay back the money he had gained in a dishonest way, did he experience peace and a special blessing. After the revival meetings were over, he took all the money he could find at home, and when it was not enough he took precious things like silver from the home and sold it so he had the sixty dollars he needed. That was a lot of money for an ordinary family. But finally when he was ready to go with that big sum, he felt happier than he had ever felt in his life. He had to walk 25 miles to the other side of the Yellow River to pay back the money. This story has spoken to many in Hequ. That a man will pay back sixty dollars in these bad times, well then—something must have happened to him.

Revival All Over China

Stories like these could be repeated all over China in the years before the 1937 Japanese invasion. I remember the names of famous Chinese people God was using, like John Sung, Watchman Nee, Wang Mingdao and members of the Bethel Band (a group of itinerant revivalists). And God used missionaries too, like Jean Graham, Elizabeth Fischbacher and Anna Christensen from the CIM, as well as Marie Monson from the Norwegian Lutheran Mission.

All over China God was preparing the church for persecution—with the Japanese war in 1937, the Communist takeover in 1949, and later the Cultural Revolution—all just around the corner. My parents and the 8,000 missionaries with them in China didn't know that they were preparing the church for these events. If they had known what was coming, they might have bungled the job of preparing the church for persecution.

The triumph lay precisely in the human limitation of not knowing the future, but in being faithful to the task God gave them to do in the present. They were caught up in something bigger than themselves—the kingdom of God—something they could not monitor. Though I was just a child, I was awed as I witnessed the coming of that kingdom in the great people's movement of new believers. In Hequ, and all over China, people bowed in worship to acknowledge and exalt the Savior of the world.

And so Mor and Far left Hequ for furlough in December 1935, unaware of the deep significance and magnitude of their and others' work. But they had a hint that the storm clouds of war were gathering. Just a month before they left, Japanese planes flew over the city of Hequ.

Peaceful
Furlough
in Norway

5

The first morning I woke up in Norway, March 12, 1936, my pigtails were tied to the bedposts. Then Edvard's grinning face appeared. I had worried about him getting sophisticated, but his pranks proved that he was still the same Edvard he had been in Hequ.

He had waited impatiently for us to arrive. It took two and one-half months to journey from Hequ to Kristiansand. First, we had taken the long journey by mule, by cart, by bus, by train and by ship to Shanghai. Two weeks later we sailed from Shanghai for Southampton, England. I will never forget it because my Sunday-school teacher for the two Sundays we had been in Shanghai came on board to bring me a lovely picture of Jesus, with children of all races snuggling on his lap.

After numerous stops on the way, we arrived in England and took the train up to London to the headquarters of the China Inland Mission. Since King George V had just died, Far's first purchase in London was three black ties for himself and his sons. Another London experience was being taken to Chissold Park by a nanny who shepherded all the little CIM missionary kids. When I took my children to see *Mary Poppins* many years later, I told them I too had a nanny who once escorted me to the park in London.

After London we had one more stop to make, in Denmark, where Far's sister Anna lived after her remarriage. Anna had been the wife of Edvard Gerard, who went to China in 1910, got tuberculosis and soon died. He had a tremendous influence in Far's life. Anna was pregnant in 1910 and was going to go to China after the baby was born, but never made it. But the China tie as well as the family tie with her continued to be very special.

But what Tante Anna remembered most about this trip was Torje, age four. He acted prim and proper in an English suit as he asked her if she wanted him to sing her a song. Of course she agreed, and then came the question, "Do you want me to sing in Norwegian, Chinese, English or German?" After six weeks on a German ship he could now add German songs to his repertoire.

Together Again As a Family

Meanwhile back in Kristiansand, with all these stops, Edvard thought we would never get home. When the boat from Denmark finally landed, he was there ahead of both customs and police. Mor wrote to friends in China about the reunion:

> It is so wonderful to meet our boy again, and you can't imagine how charming and handsome we think he is. He is also so sensible and good. When we later that evening came up to our room in my sister's house, there were the four of them in each other's arms in our big bed. Oh, it was so touching to see! And next morning there was no

discussion about who should be in Mor's arms, as the three of them usually fight about it. Now it was decided it should be Edvard and Torje. And since that day, Kari and Hakon have decided that Edvard is to have that place since he has been gone from us all so long. It was wonderful to be together again, all six of us. We rented the downstairs of a duplex, with a large garden of fruit trees, berries and flowers. The duplex was close to the sea and a dairy owned by some friends. Far would look at Mor, still thin from China, and say, "You'd better walk over to the creamery and drink some cream. That will be good for you."

Our Christian Heritage

In the process of getting to know each other, we also discovered our Christian heritage. I only remembered the extended family from pictures and letters, because I had not seen them since I was three. But soon we got reacquainted and I was deep into family history, fitting everyone into diagrams. Mormor was the easiest one to get close to because we had her semi-weekly letters read to us for over seven years.

Then there were my Torjesen grandparents, who lived across the Lund bridge. I loved to take that walk alone, especially if it rained. I absorbed the sound and smell of rain and breathed in the fresh breeze on the river. The wind could be cold and I walked briskly in my heavy rainboots, fisherman's raincoat and *sydvest* (southwester). At ten I learned to whistle in the rain.

When I got to my grandparents' house there was always a treat for me. During sunny summer days I could find my grandmother sitting outside among the blossoms and fruit trees. Ever since Far had left for China, she had founded a Hequ-prayer-and-support group that got together once a month to pray and to give toward my folks' work. She was one of our most faithful prayer supporters, and intensely interested in Hequ.

I would also often meet my aunts and cousins at the lovely white house on Ole Bull's Street, as five of the eight brothers and one sister had settled in Kristiansand. Through various members of the clan, I would hear stories of "Torje Feier" (Torje the chimney sweep), my great-grandfather who was the first one to run the family's chimney-sweeping enterprise. My brother Torje was named after him, so of course I knew about him, but never realized what a character he had been. Now I learned he would always wear a tailed coat and a short-ened version of the top hat, and look very distinguished as he met with the mayor and other leaders of the town. But he was most famous for his evangelistic endeavors. His good and rather rotund friend Bishop Christen Hoeg once told him, "You know, I think you and I should probably trade jobs," to which Torje Feier replied, "Well, I think I could do your job, but I am not sure you could manage mine. I don't think the bishop could manage to get through the chimney."

There was also the time when Torje Feier got up in the middle of the night, got dressed and prepared to depart for the hospital. His wife did what she could to get him back to bed, pleading, "Torje, you have worked hard enough all day. The night is for sleeping. Nobody needs you at the hospital at this hour." But Torje went ahead. And at the hospital door he was met by a nurse who said, "Oh, Torje, we were just hoping you would come. Here lies a poor soul dying, but he can't die. You must come and help him come to the Savior." Torje had been obedient to the inner voice, and led the patient into fellowship with his God.

One of the old-timers in Kristiansand told me that if someone was counseling one under conviction of sin and felt at a loss what to do next, the counselor would often turn to Torje Feier. "I can't do any-thing more for you, but I need to send you to Torje" had been said more than once.

Torje's wife was still alive and lived in the old house where they had entertained the dignitaries of the town. I called her Oldermor (great-grandmother), even though she was not my grandfather's mother (she had died many years before). My Oldermor was a tiny and gentle woman. When we visited her, she always served us *brus* (soda), something we had not had in China. I could imagine her in the stories I heard about Torje. Once Torje had brought the bishop home for lunch without telling Oldermor. She got him in a corner and said, "But you should tell me first. All we are having today is porridge." And he cracked in reply, "Well, if that's good enough for me, then I think it's good enough for the bishop."

Torje Feier was both a personal worker and part of that great host of lay preachers who grew out of the revival movement of that time. He traveled by horse and buggy to churches, prayer houses, school houses and private homes to hold meetings all over the county.

There was an outpouring of God's Spirit on the people of Norway at the close of the nineteenth century that resulted in a movement of male and female lay preachers who were given freedom to preach. The Lutheran state church accommodated the movement by allowing the lay leaders to build *bedehus* (prayer houses) for informal evening meetings and Sunday school, while all Christians were expected to come to the church for baptism and the regular sacraments.

In fact, two of my great-grandfathers (one from my mother's side and Torje from my father's side) were lay preachers, and had taken part in the same meeting in September 1880. My maternal great-grandfather, Kristen Hanes (after whom my brother Torje Kristen was also named), was a farmer who managed to combine farming and preaching. He would load up his organ on the back of his wagon and take off for a meeting half a day's journey away, singing and sharing the gospel. On the same page in his diary that registered that five piglets had been born that morning in the barn, he recorded that three sinners came to the Savior that night at a revival meeting, and four backsliders returned to the fold. Everything was there from when certain crops were put in and when they were harvested—when the calves were born and how much milk was sold—to where he had gone to spread the good news and who had responded to God's call. This preacher-farmer did not departmentalize life into rigid divisions of the secular and sacred.

It was one of our pleasures to spend the two summers we were furloughed at the Hanes farm, helping bring in the hay, picking the cherries, getting to know the farm animals and drinking in the atmosphere of a farm where to the third and fourth generation since my great-grandparents everyone loved the Lord. That was another great experience of discovering our Christian heritage. Mor had spent her summers at this farm with her grandparents as a little girl, so it was a home to her.

Mor's brother and sister, with their families and Mormor, all moved to the area around the farm during those summers. So we were all together as an extended family, swimming in the fjord or fishing. Mor and Far loved to fish and would often be out until late at night and come home with a boatload of cod or mackerel. The rest of the family would tease them about being God's favorite children because they often caught the most fish.

Our Chosen Poverty
It was no secret in the extended family that we were living on far less than most of our relatives. Far and Mor would discuss this openly with us children, and assure us that our simpler lifestyle was not something God had inflicted on us, but something Mor and Far had chosen for the sake of the kingdom when they became missionaries. I can never remember feeling a victim of poverty, even though we could not always buy what our cousins could. As we children cooperated with our parents' choice we were made to feel it was also our choice.

Of course this was harder to do in Norway, where we were the poor cousins, than it had been in China, where we were better off than most people around us. Yet in both countries Mor and Far set the example of not looking at our possessions in relationship to others around us, but looking at them from the perspective of a wealthy heavenly Father who would give us what we needed. In China, if the money didn't arrive at the expected time, Far would sit down at the organ and sing with his deep bass, "My Father is rich in houses and lands." Then he would throw his head back and give it all the volume he could produce in the chorus, "I'm a child of the King." And our faith as a family would rise with the volume of Far's voice.

Far also had the advantage of being brought up under the concept of chosen poverty. When his father would come home from a day in the chimney-sweep business, Far's elder sister Tes reported that he might have only six crowns in his pocket. By this time Tes was helping with the cooking for eight hungry boys, and would ask, "But don't you have more?"

"No, I couldn't take any pay. I was in the quarters of the poor today. They don't even have food to eat," he answered.

"But Far, we don't either," Tes would argue. And as she told this story to the younger generation, she would add, "Far was always like that. He was so tenderhearted. If he saw someone in need, then he would rather suffer want, than to see them suffer."

At school we played a game similar to "Rich man, Poor man," alphabetically listing all the possibilities of what we could become when we grew up. "Missionary" followed "millionaire" and of course everyone wanted to become a millionaire and teased me about being a missionary. That's when I answered them with deep conviction, but not exactly with humility, "Who of you has traveled all over the world and been to eighteen countries?" Then I would rattle off the impressive list of places I'd been, and no one dared belittle the little missionary.

There were many ways in which to compensate for our chosen poverty. Sometimes it happened without us even trying. At school we all had to have our teeth checked by the public school dentist. Since we all had such excellent teeth the dentist asked Mor what she had been feeding us in China.

"Oh, nothing unusual. We couldn't get the kind of candy you eat here for snacks, so we had grapes and goat's milk."

"That explains it," the dentist answered. "You couldn't find two better food products for good teeth."

Mor went on to explain how we had imported two sturdy Swiss goats to Hequ, by having them sit in wooden crates for five days, tied to the saddle of a mule. Then she told of Hequ's grape orchards on the Yellow River, and how we went as a family and picked grapes in abundance. Then we packed grapes in sawdust in order to have a supply for the winter. The dentist was impressed.

Pride in Our Parents

At age ten, I was gradually learning new aspects of my parents' personalities and values. After close to eight years since the last furlough, they each got a new set of clothes, bought to last. Mor came home from Rasmus Tallaksen's store, where she had once been the supervisor, with a completely new wardrobe. She looked dazzling in her new dress, hat and coat, with gloves and scarf to match. Slim and petite as she was, she wore them well, and suddenly I noticed her face with her well-shaped nose and dark eyebrows highlighting her warm blue eyes. Far was just as impressive, always looking and acting more like an athlete than a preacher. He awed our cousins in Kristiansand by walking a city block on his hands. When we visited in homes during the summer he spent time with the kids, doing cartwheels or organizing a human pyramid with himself at the bottom and little Torje at the top. I gained a new appreciation of him as I discovered how other kids enjoyed him.

If some of the adults worried about him needing to get some rest and quiet before the next meeting, he would tell the story of the traveling preacher who came to a farm where they had made great preparations to entertain him with a delicious dinner before the evening meeting. To the housewife's vast disappointment (after all her cooking) he said he never ate before he preached. Later the farmer drove the preacher to the meeting. When they came home and the preacher retired for the night, the wife asked about the sermon. The farmer replied dryly, "He may as well have eaten."

I also gained a new appreciation for Far's and Mor's public speaking. I can still remember a Sunday-morning sermon Far preached on Ecclesiastes 12:1, about remembering our Creator when we are young. As a child I was getting the message. When I visited Kristiansand in 1988, I discovered I was not the only one who remembered a sermon my father had preached. One day I met a relative who recalled a sermon Far had preached in 1937 on Psalm 16:8 ("I have set the LORD always before me. Because he is at my right hand, I will not be shaken"). Standing in the street, the ninety-year-old told me how Far lived in that verse, right in God's presence, whether he was in Norway or riding a mule in China.

Occasionally in the missionary meetings, we children were asked to sing a Chinese song. Edvard was excused, so it was just Hakon, Torje and me. I stood in the middle and sang as loud as I could, embarrassed that my younger brothers were too shy to sing loudly. So I got the idea of pinching them from the back when I wanted them to sing louder. And it worked!

Mor was also busy on furlough. She started the Nurses' Missionary Fellowship in Kristiansand. Mor already belonged to the group in Oslo, but she thought there should be local groups too. The purpose was to create community between the nurses who became missionaries and those who stayed home and supported them. One day Mor announced that all nurses interested were to come to our little home on Skippergaten. The nurse who told me the story said we did not have the twenty chairs necessary for the guests, but we had hospitality that others with bigger homes lacked. Everyone loved the event, even though they were sitting on top of each other. Mor's laughter and sunny disposition took over, and I was told, "Her spirit still lives in our group." After fifty years, they have more than 100 members.

The same nurse told me how proud Torje at age five was of his mother's medical achievements. He had gone up and down our street, Skippergaten, shouting, "My mother is the best doctor in all of China." Of course with the nearest clinic or hospital ten days' journey away, she did not have much competition!

Good Things and Endings

But as proud as we were of Mor's and Far's public performance as missionaries, what we were most happy about was who they were at home, with family and friends. On the one hand, because they had a vision beyond themselves, Mor and Far were not as preoccupied with the minutiae of life as were many adults I had noticed. Yet that perspective never detracted from them as warm individual human beings. Rather it enhanced loving personal relationships, even with those who did not want to be involved with the kingdom.

One of Far's nephews, who was then a teen-ager, remembers the kind eyes with which his uncle looked at him and put him at ease. "It wasn't a long distance to the boy inside of him," he said. "He was at once on the same wavelength with us boys. We never thought of him as an older man.

"I never felt any pressure to conform to any of his views on life," he continued. "I remember playing soccer with him in your garden and doing cartwheels. But I hated it when we were at the pier singing hymns as you left for China."

It was sad for us also as the eighteen months of furlough drew to an end. As a family we had taken many ten-mile walks together over the beautiful hills of Kristiansand, overlooking the ocean. And of course in the winter there were plenty of ski trips, as well as times we sledded.

But all good things come to an end. Soon the day dawned when it seemed like half of Kristiansand was on the pier to see us off with flowers and big red boxes of Kong Haakon candy. And there were streamers tying us to shore, hymn singing and some tears. But at home at Ole Bull's Street, Far's mother had gone to bed and was weeping alone. She always went to bed when any of her sons left home. But this time she sensed something unusual and sobbed, "I'll never see Peter again."

War
in China

6

A few days later we were pulling out of Oslo by train through Sweden and on to Germany where we would board our ship for China. On that train, and on the morning of August 8, I turned twelve. Somehow I had a sense that my carefree childhood was over. I had heard enough adult talk about the tense conditions in China to know that the future was filled with uncertainties. But we still celebrated my birthday in style. My family had gifts for me and took me to a cozy restaurant in Hamburg for my birthday party. Then in Bremen we boarded the *Scharnhorst* for the long voyage.

Meanwhile, back in Norway the mission executive had to explain in the mission publication why they had sent missionaries to a country just invaded by Japan (July 1937): "When our missionaries left on

August 6, the situation was not as serious as it is today. At that time the disturbances were limited to Beijing and Tianjin. Our plans were to avoid the areas of disturbance and go directly from Shanghai to Shanxi."

Crisis in Genoa

He went on to explain that our mission as well as the Norwegian Missionary Society had telegraphed the China-bound missionaries in Genoa, Italy, and told them they could discontinue their journey. That telegram arrived just as our ship had docked in Genoa, and we were planning our sightseeing. So the war in China was interrupting our peaceful voyage.

Each time the daily news came over the loudspeaker, we were jarred back into the reality of traveling toward war. The Japanese, with their well-armed troops and modern aircraft, were moving quickly toward cities with names too close to heart and home to ignore. By contrast, the Mediterranean had spelled nothing but peace, with barely a quiver on the shiny glass-like expanse. I stood by the rail for hours and guarded the stillness.

As Mor and Far and the other Norwegians met for prayer and consultation in one of the larger cabins, the stillness seemed to be broken. Should they return to Norway? Or should they go into the unknown where there was war?

Meanwhile we kids huddled together on deck to share our fears. Would we get killed? On the other hand, wouldn't it be a letdown just to go back to Norway? Like interrupting an adventure before it began!

In the grown-up huddle some similar fears were voiced. Mor and Far did not say much, but encouraged their friends to verbalize their apprehensions. It was good to get it out in a circle where all shared the same faith and the same fears. There was some vacillation, but as they talked it out it was remembered that all the missionaries had a vision beyond themselves or their safety and private goals. War or not, they still had their vision to penetrate China for the kingdom. Perhaps they felt like us kids. They might miss the greatest adventure of their lives if they turned back. Jesus' call in Luke 9:62 was also quoted and became the obvious answer to their dilemma: "No one who puts his hand to the plow and looks back is fit for service in the kingdom of God."

So when the *Scharnhorst* pulled out of Genoa all the Norwegian missionaries were still on board and bound for China. After the decision had been made, everyone relaxed and enjoyed the journey. Five weeks on the sea, with stops in many ports, was always accepted gratefully as the bonus of our checkered missionary adventures. With parties for kids on board, swimming and lots of chums, and Mor going to dinner every night in a long dress, looking like a queen, arm-in-arm with her king, I remember wishing the journey would never end. But it did. However, not before we had enjoyed riding elephants in Colombo, Sri Lanka, and seen the beautiful sights of Medan on Sumatra.

Then came Manila, where the journey ended abruptly for half the passengers. It seemed like panic gripped people when they heard the news of the Japanese advance in China. We went on to disembark in Hong Kong, rather than Shanghai as planned, and took the train to Hankow (now part of Wuhan) in Hubei, on the Yangtze River. Edvard remembers how from the train we could see young soldiers waiting to cross the river. Many wore bloody bandages and most were bone thin, their drawn faces filled with fear. One soldier on a stretcher was moaning in his pain, but all the comfort he received was a kick from his officer. The reality of war hit us.

In Hankow we suffered our first air raid. First we stood on the roof and watched the planes trying to bomb the ships in the river. As kids we had always loved to watch Chinese firecrackers explode. But this was different—the bombs were gigantic firecrackers, dazzling us with their light and deafening us with their din. We guarded every ship in the river with our transfixed gaze, and were relieved that none of them was hit, to explode into pieces before our eyes. Instead the bombs plunged into the river and exploded harmlessly.

As the bombers left the river and flew toward us, we were all called to go under the stairs for shelter in the CIM home where we were boarding. All the booming noises were new to me. I had never heard anything before so loud and deafening. The roaring din of the many planes overhead would suddenly be drowned out by the ear-piercing thunder of a bomb exploding somewhere, sounding as if it were happening right next door. I recall the din and the thuds, and then the thought that above those planes there was the Father in heaven who still cared for us.

South to Peach Blossom Hill

Shanxi was embroiled in the conflict with Japan and it was soon evident that it was no place to take four children. But God had already prepared a new way. While on the *Scharnhorst* our Norwegian Missionary Society friends had invited us to their Norwegian school in Hunan if we couldn't make it to the Norwegian school in Shanxi. And so we took the train south to Changsha, and from there to Daohwalun (Peach Blossom Hill), where the Norwegian school was located. Since there were no boarding facilities at that time, this decision meant Mor would have to attend to us children, while Far explored the possibilities of going to Shanxi alone. He spent hours poring over the newspapers to see if there was any route into Shanxi where the fighting was less intense.

While Far waited to hear from colleagues who might advise him how and where to travel, God opened a door of ministry for him on Peach Blossom Hill. One of the missionaries wrote about it for *Evangelisten,* a popular Christian periodical in Norway:

We were glad to have Torjesen and his family with us. . . . But we could see that the missionary in him was not totally content. . . . Then one day we woke up to the sound of trumpets and fanfare. The troops were coming through on their way to the front with shining helmets. Another day, another group of soldiers—but no shining helmets and no fanfare. They were wounded and tattered, dirty and tired. One had a bandage on his head. Another no arm. Another was limping along on his crutches—coming from the front.

The next group that came to town was the refugees—women and children, old and young. They were tired and dirty and ragged— driven from their homes and their rice-fields. Their loved ones had been killed by the Japanese, or trampled under foot in the mass exodus as thousands had fled from the war zone. Now they were alone among strangers in a strange province.

Most of the wounded soldiers and refugees from the North could not understand the Hunan dialect. But Torjesen they understood. Suddenly he became another person. We got a glimpse of the real missionary inside him. Early and late he was busy. We could see him surrounded by a group of soldiers listening to his simple testimony. Next he was inside an ancestral hall where hundreds of refugees were looking for some type of shelter. Next at the temple by the river to visit the Buddhist monks also in flight.

His good smile brought courage to all as he spoke words of comfort to each person. There might be a tract given, or just a word about the Lord he loved. Quietly and with great inner freedom he moved among these people. This is how I remember him—always ready to comfort and help—eager to give the Good News, and filled with the missionary joy over the slightest sign of new life sprouting.

But eventually Far left us and this new ministry to try to get back to Hequ. He got as far as Henan, the province south of Shanxi, and stayed there with Lutheran friends, again working with wounded soldiers. The good part about him not having made it to Hequ was that he came back to Peach Blossom Hill to enjoy Christmas with us. On the way he stopped in Hankow to pick up all our luggage from the *Scharnhorst,* which hadn't arrived when we left Hankow earlier. We were cold in the Hunan December without our winter clothes, so Far's arrival was a double blessing.

Mor wrote home to her mother,

We are so grateful to God for letting us once more be together as a family for Christmas. And what fun to unpack things we hadn't seen since we left Norway. You all became so dear to us as we found things you had sent with us. It is good to feel loved and carried on the arms of prayer in these times. Everything added to our Christmas festivity. New clothes we all got, and things we need for the house. And goat cheese, Norwegian sausage and chocolate . . . It is amazing that the children are not more plagued by the fear of war. This is God's doing. They constantly hear the news about the war and see the wounded soldiers on the roads.

So in spite of the war we had a perfect Christmas. With Far having brought the trunks from Norway, there were plenty of decorations for the house and the tree. Peach Blossom Hill also had several evergreens, so we had pine branches over the doors and windows and on the floor at the entrance, as in an old Norwegian farm house. For the holiday, we invited parents whose children were in school in Norway and lonely husbands whose wives had gone to Norway with the children (to spare them from war). All these loved to be with a happy family with four children. Far kept them all entertained with his stories, and then would suddenly surprise them with talking about the Lord, as naturally as he had told his jokes. One of the young missionaries told how awed he was by the ease with which Far spoke about the Lord.

Far Returns to Hequ

After a warm family Christmas, Far again spent some days with the wounded soldiers and refugees. But his heart was back in Hequ and that was his goal in January 1938. He made it to Shanxi by the Chinese New Year, and wrote to the mission:

It is good to find that among our missionaries as well as other missions, most have chosen to stay at their posts instead of evacuating. They have chosen to stay to suffer with the people. I am so grateful to be back here. The last four months I have been in Hunan and Henan and tried to help with the work, mostly among wounded soldiers. Everytime I met one from Shanxi it was like meeting a fellow-citizen. . . . The trip North went well. One night on the train I sat up with the soldiers and answered questions about the Gospel as long as I could. They did not seem to get tired.

The soldiers would ask, "How do you know that your God is the true God?" Far would then get his well-worn Chinese Bible and read to them from Genesis 1, with the soldiers crowding around to follow the text. After many questions about creation, Far would go on with the story of the fall and the need for a Savior. With constant discussion, that would take another few hours. Then he got to the story of the cross. At this point, one of the soldiers would think that it is going too far for a mighty God to die on a cross and would ask, "Why can't we just live good lives according to Confucian law?" That would lead to some concrete examples of how sinful we are, even when we want to do what is right. And so the night passed.

Meanwhile, at Peach Blossom Hill Mor was surprised that Far had even made it to Shanxi, and wrote home, "Since Shanxi is in the war zone it was impossible to get a pass, but at the Eighth Army Headquarters in Hankow he got some medicines to bring for the Linfen hospital, along with a letter of introduction. . . . It's the Eighth Army which is now in charge in Shanxi."

After more waiting we heard that Far had arrived safely in Hequ. But for Mor the hardest trial after that was no mail for six weeks following. I remember daily looking for a letter from him. Then on April Fool's Day, 1938, we pulled a thoughtless trick on her and brought a letter with an enthusiastic, "It is from Far." I never felt so wicked in my life as when I saw her disappointed face. Of course, Mor later forgave us.

In May she wrote to Kristiansand,

The children and I wondered how Far was doing in the middle of the war. He could be dead for all we knew. For three weeks we read daily in the news about Hequ and the war there. But after Easter when the letters began to come we heard how Peter arrived just in time—before the road was closed because of the Japanese advance.

It was so exciting to read about Peter's arrival in Hequ. The congregation had called Baote the day before to be sure when he was coming. As he came riding towards Hequ, he met one delegation after another on the road. And when he got to the big gate on top of the hill—another group was waiting for him—where the view is so breathtaking with the city below and the Yellow River winding its way like a silver thread through the foliage. Further down the hill the women with their bound feet were waiting, and still further down on the plain waited the dear old women who walk with sticks. What a joyful reunion! At the church a big feast was ready, and after the meal a thanksgiving service. You can understand why all this makes me lonesome for Hequ.

Far continues the story for the mission:

First came the crisis in February when 3,000 Japanese soldiers took the city. The defeated Chinese troops plundered everything they could before escaping over the river. But in the middle of this confusing time we had the most wonderful opportunity to minister to the three hundred refugees who sought shelter with us. It would not have been an easy time for the Chinese Christians to be alone. For example, one day a Japanese officer came and demanded three young Chinese girls [to use as prostitutes]. When he got a very definite refusal from me, he gave up and walked away ashamed.

All these reports made Mor homesick for Far and Hequ, wishing she could be there to share in all the experiences. But Mor also knew how to make the best out of life where she was. One of the highlights for her that spring was her visits to the hospital to comfort the wounded soldiers. Most of them were from the north, and she spoke their dialect. Because Mor needed someone to go with her and one of the missionaries, Antonie Hagen, was interested, this became their joint project. But at first Antonie wondered if women should be the ones to go and visit sick soldiers. Traditionally she had thought of this as a job for a male chaplain. She writes about this conflict and Mor's personality in her excellent book, *Life and Suspense in China:*

"This really should be men's work," I said to Mrs. Torjesen.

"Far from it," she replied. "These rough men are much more ready to open up to us women. We remind them of Mother at home."

Mor saw herself as a mother to anyone who needed mothering. She was delighted when these young men, so far away from home, responded to her. In a way, she was going against the culture for the higher value of meeting the needs of these men where they hurt most.

As we finished our school year at the Norwegian School on Peach Blossom Hill at the end of May, there had been talk of going to Chefoo to meet Far for a family summer vacation. But that May Far had received more than 1,000 refugees at the station in Hequ. There were air raids every day for ten days, and the Japanese forces were just a few miles from the city when God answered prayer and they turned to go another way. But with war also came the typhus and typhoid epidemic among the refugees, spread by the wounded soldiers that civilians were supposed to take in and nurse to health. Far wrote that there were already 100 cases in Hequ. Some of the afflicted were staying at the church. Concerned for his health, one of the older Christian women leaders kept saying to Far, "Don't go near the sick room. Your life is too precious."

Far wrote, "But I still had to handle the responsibility of helping the sick to move back where they came from when the emergency was over. The day after God sent a blessed rain. It poured for a day and a half and washed away all the garbage left after 1,000 refugees had stayed with us. It was also good for the farmers. This year people need a good crop to survive."

During this time of upheaval and fear, when they needed him most, the leaders of the congregation came and asked Far not to leave them for the summer vacation in Chefoo. He also saw the many open doors and open hearts to respond to the gospel at such a time and decided it was God's will for him to stay.

So instead of going to Chefoo to meet Far as planned, we went to a summer place at Tienchaoping up in the mountains, literally above the clouds, where the Norwegian Missionary Society had its summer retreat. We had a wonderful summer with this Christian community.

The School Evacuates
Meanwhile, the war was coming to Hunan, and during our time on the mountain the Norwegian Missionary Society decided to evacuate the school and all women with children to Hong Kong. Of course we were included. First we had to get to Changsha, the capital. Since all vehicles were needed for the war, we could not get regular transportation and were smuggled under the tarp of a truck on its way to pick up supplies. It was like being part of a mystery. As we giggled one moment and complained the next, there were lots of hushed scoldings from the grownups. They were far more tense about the situation than we were.

When we boarded the train in Changsha for Hong Kong, we sobered up. The reality of war hit us again. We went through some times of frightened prayers to God to take care of us as the Japanese planes were trying to bomb our train. How we thanked God when we reached a tunnel where we hid for hours, until the planes had given up on us. When we reached Hong Kong the first news that greeted us was that the Japanese had burned Changsha. Again we thanked God for getting us out just in time.

In Hong Kong there was another Christian community to receive us. At first we stayed at the Basel Mission and had our school at the Norwegian Seaman's Mission. When school was in session, the Norwegian flag was out for all to see.

During our first months in Hong Kong, Far finally came to see us. I wrote about the visit in a composition for school:

One day we came home from school and saw suitcases, and from the next room we heard laughter and fun. It couldn't be Far who had arrived? He who is so far away. But when we entered the next room there he stood in the middle and received one hug and kiss after the other. Oh, I was so happy! . . . There were a thousand things to tell. All that had happened to us and to Far during the ten months we had been apart. . . . There was no end to all he had experienced. . . . And then he had something with him for all of us—a big carton full. The first evening we were all up late.

The days went and soon we knew Far had to leave us again. But before he left we had a last day together. First we went to see the monkeys and had lots of fun. Later we went to the beach. There was nothing like swimming with Far. He was full of acrobatic feats as usual, turning cartwheels and walking on his hands, and having us dive off his shoulder in the sea. We all swam with him out to a big ship far out in the ocean. Afterwards we had ice cream, and so the last day with Far was over.

What I didn't say in my composition was that this event was the first time I had seen Far lose his cool with a Chinese. Usually he was all politeness to the Chinese, and they were courteous to him. But the man at the gate to the beach club had his own sophisticated way about him, a way that took Far off guard. When the man quoted the price of admission, Far, forgetting this was a British colony, started to bargain by asking for a lower price. After all, during his twenty years in China Far had always bargained every time he took out his billfold. Why not now? And having just come from war-torn Shanxi, where a bowl of boiled millet was appreciated as if it had been a banquet, paying such a high fee to swim seemed almost immoral. But to the British-trained guard at the gate, a foreigner who bargained at a beach club needed to be put in his place. At this point Far lost his cool and let the guard know the price was too high.

I have no memory of his behavior embarrassing me before this, as I had grown up with the secure philosophy that my parents always did what they did because that would be best for us all. Far hadn't changed; I had. I had just turned thirteen. But Far regained his cool, paid the standard fee and rejoined us to enjoy the day at the beach.

Not too long after Far had returned to Hequ, we moved to the Christian Buddhist Mission on Taofongshan, near Shatin station. The missionaries had a house for us where we crowded together—three mothers, our teacher and seven children. But we had a great time of Christian togetherness.

Though we were called refugees from war-torn China, we had a good year in Hong Kong. Every other Sunday the Norwegian Lutheran seaman's pastor invited us to a worship service, then for lunch in a restaurant and finally a swim in the bay. He knew that on our missionary salary we could afford neither the lunch nor the fee to get into the Lido Beach Club, so he called us his team to minister to the Norwegian seamen and paid the bill. With great warmth he assured us that we were more than paying for ourselves by being a Christian presence before the sailors, who seldom saw Christian family life when away from home. We never dreamt "having a ministry" could be so much fun.

Alone in Hequ

Meanwhile Far was having a different type of fun as he watched with great satisfaction the Christians doing the work of the ministry. During the severe bombings anywhere from 300 to more than 1,000 people lived on the church premises, and he wrote, "We have prayed with many of them, but perhaps the best work is done by the Christians who live together with the refugees . . . day after day, and seek to help them to God. In the evening we can often hear prayer and singing in the various rooms."

In his annual report for 1938, Far wrote:

It has been a year of light and shadows. I have never seen such progress in the work of the Kingdom, nor such dark clouds. . . . In the fall the Japanese began again to bomb Hequ and Pianguan. One reason is that the generals Fu Tso-yi and Ma Chan have their headquarters near these cities. Our station was recently hit, but no people were hurt. We had good conferences both in Hequ and Pianguan, where we have visited for the past ten years, but only now we see results. . . . We now have an evangelist couple living there who have the people's confidence. . . . In Hequ we have had meetings in the street chapel every night. The church has grown with thirty-five baptisms this year. . . . Both in the work in Hequ and on the long journeys to and from the field we have sensed the Unseen Power opening doors step by step.

This report was enclosed in a personal letter to me from Far, with instructions to have Mor send it airmail to Norway. He was so grateful to have received letters from his children on December 23. Separated as Far was from all of us that Christmas, at least he got our letters on time. But he did not tell me about his Christmas. Instead he told me about my friends in Hequ who were faithful in coming to church, and all the children who stopped him on the street to ask when the Sunday-school Christmas fest would be. The Christians were busy making preparations with packages of fruit and nuts and *ma-tang* (my favorite Chinese candy, made of molasses and sesame seeds) for each child. He also wrote that fellow missionaries, living two days distant, had sent a horse so Far could travel and spend New Year's with them. But Far said he could not leave. How he loved the people of Hequ.

Our School Crisis

Meanwhile, as we started our Christmas holidays in Hong Kong, we realized we were the last students left in the school. Because of the war, students had either not returned from Norway, or been evacuated. So the school we had loved so much had to close by that summer, 1939. For two years we had been inspired by the most wonderful teacher in the world. Edvard said about her, "I doubt if any teacher has influenced me so much," and I echo his sentiments. She had the rare combination of being totally involved in her subject matter and simultaneously in her student. Loving history, she could make King Olaf II (995?-1030) come alive—while all the time she was looking into my eyes as if teaching me and nurturing me was the most important thing in her life.

Now Mor had to make a decision without the benefit of discussing it with Far, since the mail was slow and a decision was due soon. Where should we continue our schooling? In Hong Kong? Or in Chefoo? Of course she wrote volumes of letters to Far about it all, but by the time he got them and answered, she had already been forced to make the decision. Both choices would mean switching from Norwegian to English as the medium of instruction. All this we discussed and

92

prayed about with her, as we were all aware of the heaviness and uncertainty in Mor's spirit. She spent much time on her knees, or took long slow walks alone. While she talked freely about the decision to others, she knew that finally she had to hear "the still small voice" all on her own.

She emerged from some heavy weeks to announce that Chefoo seemed the right choice. It was the CIM school, with a deep commitment to both the spiritual growth and the academic excellence of the students. Mor also reminded us that she and Far had agreed that we should not be in a place where the war was going on. Though Chefoo was in China, it was in Japanese-occupied territory where there was no fighting. Chefoo had been described as "situated on the curve of a quiet bay with a Yellow Sea-front and a range of hills behind it, a haven of peace for generations of missionaries' children."

Our Last Summer Together

Once more we left a wonderful Christian community in Hong Kong to join another in Chefoo. We knew few people when we arrived in Chefoo by ship, but were immediately received as family. The family of God was very much alive in China in those days of war.

Far arrived from Hequ a week after we came to Chefoo. Again we were grateful for the gift of family, which we had now learned not to take for granted. And with the gift of each other, God also gave us a beautiful summer cottage in which to enjoy our reunion. Mor wrote home to her mother about it:

It is Sunday afternoon and the bay lays quiet and peaceful before us. We can see big and small boats that add to the sense of peace. It is strange to be living in such a troubled land, and yet how grateful we are to God for this wonderful summer he has given us. The best thing is that we are once more together as a family. God was so good to bring Peter to us, and he has also taken care of the pressure Peter has been under in the war zone so that it has not depressed him. . . . [The cottage] is up high with the most gorgeous view. It reminds us so much of dear Kristiansand. The house is like a little cottage in the country. We have it all to ourselves, so once more we have a home like we had when we were in Norway. But now we are already in the middle of August so too soon these two months in this peaceful home will come to an end . . . once more we have to face separation.

We enjoyed our times at home in the cottage and daily went swimming in the ocean. Much of the time Mor was busy sewing four children's outfits for four different seasons, plus name tags on every stitch of clothing. Meanwhile, Far took us to the beach to swim, as well as to the activities for children and young people on the beach. Alone at home, Mor dreaded the separation from us. For the past two years she had not only faced the conflict between her calling as a mother and as a missionary, but an even more complicated conflict between the desires to be with her husband or with her children.

Now we were entering a British boarding-school where 300 children were away from their parents. While Mor saw this provision as the answer to her prayers to return to Hequ with Far, it did not make the separation easier. At one point she actually explored the possibility of renting a home and staying with us. But this plan was scrapped as she thought of the man she loved and shared a common call with, and who had already been separated from her for almost two years.

For both Mor and Far life in wartime China did not give them neat uncomplicated choices. They both knew that they would smart under the separation from their children. But they also knew that to bring us into the war zone in Shanxi would be wrong. At the same time they realized we were closer than we had ever been as a family and wistfully wished the idyllic life could continue.

But we were a family of pilgrims on the move for God. While we all busied ourselves with packing for school and closing up the cottage, subconsciously we kids were absorbing some of Mor's and Far's vision of the kingdom beyond us. As they talked of Hequ as the place God had called them to, we knew deep inside that we could not ask them to ignore that call. All these unformulated concepts were still under the surface as we faced our separation, while each day we were grateful for one more day together, clinging to each other, as the parting day drew closer. There were many spontaneous hugs, and quite a few tears we could not hold back, even when we tried to be brave about it.

The parting was hardest for Hakon. He was going into fifth grade in an English school without ever having had English as a foreign language in the Norwegian school. But it was more than the language problem. Suddenly he started overturning suitcases that were packed and ready to be closed. He challenged Mor, "God made you to be my mother, and therefore you must stay." Mor smarted under the words. Who could argue with his logic? This outburst didn't make the parting any easier.

We met as a pilgrim family for the last time on September 2, 1939, to read Psalm 121, the traveler's psalm we had always read before trips: "The LORD will watch over your coming and going both now and forevermore." It was an eternal promise for Mor and Far to cling to as they knew they had to leave us.

Peter Torjesen shortly before his departure for China, 1918.

Right: Valborg and Peter at their wedding in Lan Xian, January 17, 1923. Below: At the Torjesens' first home in Hequ, Valborg studies Chinese with a tutor.

New missionaries Valborg and Peter enjoy a Chinese meal with Norwegian colleagues at the Sommerly retreat.

Peter and Valborg with Edvard and Kari at Sommerly in 1926.

One-year-old Kari and two-year-old Edvard prepare to travel by donkey, with Valborg leading.

Edvard, Kari and Hakon at Sommerly, 1930.

Hakon, Torje and Kari in their yard at Hequ, 1932.

Hakon, Kari and Torje travel to the coast on a one-eared mule.

The last family portrait, made in Norway, 1937.

Left: Valborg in 1956, while touring Norway with Hakon.
Below: The four Torjesen children at a 1982 reunion, with spouses: Edvard (with Jenny), Kari (with Bob Malcolm), Hakon (with Karen) and Torje (with Reidun).

No Cost
Is Too
Great

7

After we had prolonged all the goodbye ceremonies and wiped our
tears more than once, Mor and Far got into their rickshaws and we
reached up for one last kiss. Edvard was fifteen, I was fourteen, Hakon
eleven and Torje seven. We waved unenthusiastically as they headed
down San Lane toward the ship that was to take them to Tianjin. Then
we mechanically stepped inside the compound gate, and looking over
the brick wall, caught one more glimpse of our parents, their heads
bobbing to the rhythm of the rickshaws. It was then I knew that that
was the last time I would see them together.

This knowledge was like a delicate secret that came from deep inside
of me. I didn't immediately think of it as God speaking to me, but later
I identified it with the "still small voice." It wasn't a frightening ex-

perience, but a quiet inner certainty, wrapped in the greater certainty of God's unlimited love for us as a family.

When Mor and Far reached Beijing, a letter from Hakon was waiting for them. In it he wrote about having it out with the Almighty, in a sort of Job-like fashion, after he went to bed the first night he was without them. God had spoken to him tenderly about being like a loving parent to him. Next morning he was ready to write to them, "Jesus is now my father, so it is alright for you to leave me."

At evening prayers at school, the night Mor and Far left, we sang the hymn "I Need Thee Every Hour, Most Gracious Lord." Never had I needed someone infinitely bigger than me as much as I needed God right then. I knew our family life would never be the same again. The four of us had already had our lives turned upside down because of the Japanese war. Now we were in a British boarding-school with English as the medium of instruction. Edvard and I had studied English earlier, but Hakon and Torje didn't even have conversational English as they began to compete in the classroom. The language problem didn't make it any easier to separate from Mor and Far.

I faced the separation from another perspective when I wrote to my grandmother in Norway that fall: "We are here now in Chefoo alone, and expecting a good Christmas, though it will be the first time away from home. It says in Matthew 19:29 that all who are away from family for God's sake will receive a special reward. . . . That's what keeps me going."

Going to Shanxi

Meanwhile, Mor and Far reached Beijing just in time to hear the reports of all the cities in Shanxi that had just been taken. The next destination for the Japanese was Hequ. Many of the missionaries who had evacuated Shanxi thought it was hopeless to get through the enemy lines, and said it was best not even to try in such a critical time.

The missionaries from England had been forced to leave because of the anti-English stance of the Japanese. But this only added to the sense of urgency among the Scandinavians to remain in their posts. None of the Scandinavian countries were yet involved in World War 2 (which started in Europe in September 1939). This gave the Scandinavian missionaries neutral status with the Japanese.

"The responsibility seems to rest more on us Norwegians and Swedes than earlier, now that the way is closed for the others, and we are the only ones who can get permits to go inland," my parents wrote to the mission in Norway. And so amidst outward tension and the inward drive to reach Hequ, Mor and Far went to the highest Japanese authorities in Beijing to ask for a pass.

"We are good friends with Norway," said the official. "It's a small country. And what's the name of the man who wrote *Peer Gynt?*" Before they had time to answer, he wrote down "Henrik Ibsen." Mor and Far were impressed.

"And then the other—Synnove Solbakken?" their Japanese friend continued, "Oh yes, Bjornstjerne Bjornsen." And he wrote these names down on the pad. "In my country we have the collected works of both authors translated into Japanese. But the Chinese don't," he said proudly. Then he gave Mor and Far passes all the way to Hequ.

Arriving in Shanxi

Mor and Far didn't waste any time boarding the train for Shanxi. From Datong, on September 20, 1939, they wrote to the mission in Norway,

> Now we have finally reached good old Shanxi. . . . Our prayer is that if it is in agreement with God's will, that God will open doors for us all the way to Hequ, and once more allow us to work among the dear ones in that place, and seek to win new converts in the time that is left. . . . We also feel that the doors will be closed for us here

in China—maybe sooner than we had thought.

After taking the train to the end of the line in Ningwu, Shanxi, they had four more days to go. Though most mules were taken for the war, miraculously a man with two mules offered to take them to Hequ. But after two days, when they reached Shenchi (the last outpost under Japanese rule) the mule-drivers were frightened and refused to go on. Mor wrote home to Norway,

> Houses were deserted and the city wall partly torn down. The main street of town—usually a lively place—was like the place for the dead. There wasn't a Chinese in sight—only the guards in the foreign uniforms. As we moved on we found the houses were nearly all in ruins due to bombing. . . . As the guards stopped us on our lonely pilgrimage they were amazed that we were on our way to Hequ where there were so many Chinese troops. We soon discovered that we could find neither an inn nor a private family who would take us in for the night. So we went out the city gate on the north side into the open countryside. There came a farmer who helped us to find a deserted house in ruins. We put up our camp cots in a shed that once had been a home for a family. Now everything was deserted. We could get neither food, nor water, nor heat. The mud-stove was also torn up. The worst was when the mule-drivers put our things down and told us they did not dare cross the lines to the Chinese side.

Needing Donkeys to Reach Hequ

"It did not look bright for us," Mor continued.

> Where would we get animals to ride in such a deserted place? But we knew God would take care of us. He had never let us down. . . . After a few hours a man came with a kettle and we got boiling water. A little later the same man came with noodles in a wash basin! We thanked God for the food, and it went down without

thinking too much about the wash basin or the man's paralyzed hand. (Chinese don't usually serve food in a wash basin, nor does a man with a paralyzed hand usually serve food, but this is war time!) But after he was gone and we were trying to settle for the night, we felt the depressing stillness even more intensely. The town and the landscape around were so deserted. The only life we saw was the foreign guard up on the city wall, whom we could see clearly in the eerie moonlight. But after we again committed our situation to the Lord, we went to sleep immediately.

Later we were awakened in the night by the mule-driver who had left us earlier. He came to tell us that out in the country he had found some farmers with donkeys willing to take us to Hequ. . . . We are sure this man was sent by God to help us even though he didn't dare go himself. But he had it on his heart to help us. May God bless and reward this man. With thanksgiving in our hearts we left this critical place quietly, along the city wall until we came to the mountains beyond, and after having passed one more Japanese guard-post, we were finally in Chinese territory again.

Riding into Hequ

After two tiresome days riding on weak, famished little donkeys (since no mules were available), Mor and Far triumphantly entered their beloved Hequ on September 30, 1939. Nobody expected them, as the Christians had almost given up hope of their ever getting through the enemy lines. But once the word was out that the missionaries were home, the festivities began.

Mor wrote to us at boarding school about their homecoming: "What great joy! We arrived in the afternoon just as they had started the prayer meeting at church. A lot of the faithful women were there. After the meeting they all came to see us, and you can imagine the jubilation. The neighbors also came running. All were so glad to see us."

107

Though Mor was especially tired and sore from the day's ride on that tiny donkey, something she was not used to, there was no rest until everyone had a chance to talk with them. And Sunday became another feast day as the church was overcrowded both morning and afternoon. The celebration continued.

But other aspects of the homecoming were less joyful. To Mor, who hadn't been there since furlough, it was a different Hequ. "The war had taken its toll on both the people and the land," she wrote home to Norway.

The first thing that struck me was the gnawing silence as if the city had been forsaken. Many have deserted it for out-of-the-way places in the country-side, and others have fled north of the Great Wall to Inner Mongolia. . . . Those who are left experience continued angst over the possibility of Japanese planes coming to drop bombs. . . . Tumbled down homes and ruins are seen everywhere in the city. On Main Street business has ceased and the bigger stores are closed. Only late in the afternoon there are some small shops that open. . . . And with war comes pestilence. For two years typhus and typhoid epidemics have been rampant in nearly every village around Hequ. . . . Whole families laid there sick and died due to neglect because no one dared to help the sick for fear of contagion.

She goes on to describe both famine and drought, and the heavy burden on the people to feed the Chinese troops stationed in Hequ, when they didn't have enough to feed their own mouths. After all the bad news, she returns again to their flock of believers who in their first month back enjoyed the fall rally for three days with a full house, and extended the fellowship to a fourth day.

The Gospel Hall in the main part of town was open again, and the people in general around town were showing their appreciation that Mor and Far were back among them. Many of these were among the 1,000 and more who found shelter at the church during the heaviest

108

bombing raids by the Japanese when Far was alone. People had nowhere else to go during the emergency, and the large two-storied house and bomb shelter at the church gave them a sense of security. Mor closes the letter with a reference to Luke 19:44. She longs to see people's hearts open to the Lord, that they might "know the time of (their) visitation" (NKJV).

Disturbing News

On December 12, 1939, Mor wrote to her mother about a personal trial only a mother could understand:

We have only heard from the children once since we got home. . . . That was the time when the eighty-year-old man took the four-day trip and returned with a whole bunch of letters from them. What a feast that was! But that's the only time. Then we got a telegram two weeks ago that Torje had diphtheria, but is doing well. Yes, there has been quite a few trials, and that's the way we felt about this, but . . . nothing happens without the Lord permitting it. He is our refuge under all circumstances.

It's good to know the children are in safe hands and that our friends are doing everything they can for them. But when sickness comes we would like to be close to them. That's the way I feel now. We hope Torje will be better so he can leave the hospital by Christmas. . . . Winter vacation lasts for them through December and January. Most children travel home then, but for us it was impossible this year. Now it is soon Christmas, but we don't know if we can get anyone to fetch their letters in time. They are in Ningwu on the Japanese side, but it's hard to get through the lines. And especially now that Torje is sick and we don't know anymore, we are waiting for letters.

Yet, undaunted, on the same day she wrote in another letter, "It is so good as long as the doors are open and we can work unhindered. We

109

feel as if . . . maybe the time after this will be short." Far had expressed a similar sentiment in an earlier letter home to Norway: "There are many who think that soon foreigners will not get permission to live and work in Shanxi province. But that is in God's hand. May we work as long as the opportunity is there."

These letters were written in the run-down, mud-brick house in which we had lived since I was a little girl. Every year it had to be repaired. It had no foundation—just the mud bricks, a few wooden beams and a flat roof. Worst of all, Far could not even dig a bomb shelter. Mor wrote to Norway, "Peter tried to excavate for a shelter, but found the water level was too near the surface. Therefore it was impossible to dig more than a few feet into the ground without water rising into the hole, causing the soil to cave in. On the other hand, the bomb shelter at the church is in good condition."

In one of his letters home in early 1939, Far had written about this bomb shelter:

I was part of the crew that worked hard on that for three weeks. We got free bricks. The old beautiful city wall of Hequ was being torn down in order not to give protection to the Japanese when they come. These bricks are five times as big as modern bricks and much stronger. This was a real provision for us who wanted solid material to make the shelter safe from bombs. Interestingly enough, we hit bedrock 20 feet under the ground, so now the foundation will also be solid. This gave the believers a new sense of security, even though there will only be room for women and children if many people come.

The Bombing and the Ministry

During that last year there were many references in Far's correspondence to hours spent in the bomb shelter, "packed like sardines in a can." In his last letter to the mission, he wrote,

Yesterday we were again down in the bomb shelter. We sat there for over half an hour while three planes threw 20 bombs. . . . One wonders why they continue to bomb this defenceless city . . . [with] no more soldiers in the town, just a few troops spread around the mountains. . . . Many people continue to leave town. . . . for Inner Mongolia and settle on a piece of land. Also many of the believers are leaving us. We sometimes wish we could go with and work among the refugees from Hequ. They even have the railway up there [Inner Mongolia]. But we need to stay at our post.

It was not easy to come back to Hequ this time. Our house needed repair so we could live in it one more winter. Hope to be able to buy a place soon. This house which is ready to tumble down is not worth the annual rent the mission is paying for it.

In the ministry everything is going well. Valborg has begun daily classes for men and women. Many come to the Sunday meetings, especially in the afternoon when they are not afraid of planes. When the planes came yesterday the Sunday school had just gathered. It was good that there were only about fifty children, so there was room for all in the bomb shelter. There they stood together— some crying and some praying. The believers have many experiences of answered prayer these days. We had testimonies yesterday from three young men who were thrown in prison by the Japanese and almost shot. One had been a prisoner for 17 months. In his need he cried to God and was set free. Through this their faith has been greatly strengthened.

But one thing Far did not write home about was an incident that took place while he was at Chefoo with us that past summer. The Chinese military of the Nationalist government had asked to use the church for a meeting. And the evangelist in charge had felt that he had no power to refuse them. When Mor and Far heard about this it obviously made them uneasy, but there was nothing they could do about it. They also

111

knew what military pressure meant and how vulnerable the evangelist was in the face of it.

But when the Japanese intelligence found out about this later, there were two to three weeks of air attacks, aimed exactly at the mission station. The fact that the civilian refugees and wounded soldiers found refuge at the mission station was also reported by spies to the Japanese, who thus saw the missionaries as supporters of the Chinese people against their invaders. Mor and Far no longer had the protection that was promised to those from neutral countries like Norway.

December 14, 1939

But Mor and Far were totally unaware of the change of attitude toward them by the Japanese, as they put out the Norwegian flag on December 14—flat on the ground to make it as visible as possible to the enemy planes in the sky. This had become as much of a routine each day as eating breakfast and reading the verse for the day on the calendar. As they stood there hand in hand before the calendar that day, they read the verse and reread it to each other: "As the heavens are higher than the earth, so are my ways higher than your ways" (Is 55:9).

For Far there was some deep hidden meaning in that verse, Mor told us. In his quiet way he discussed with her how we have to reach the place of commitment where we can accept God's ways. Together they prayed that as servants of the Most High they would seek God's agenda, not their own.

Sometime later that day Far, as we remember him doing often, went to the little pump organ that had travelled with them to Hequ, and played and sang hymns of praise. Mor could never forget that that day he sang in Norwegian, *"Takk min Gud for alt som hende."* Especially significant was the stanza:

Thanks for prayers that Thou hast answered

112

Thanks for what Thou dost deny
Thanks for home and thanks for fireside
Thanks for hope that sweet refrain!
Thanks for joy and thanks for sorrow
Thanks for heavenly peace with Thee!
Thanks for hope in the tomorrow,
Thanks through all eternity.

The rest of the day was filled with its regular routine. Far had just returned the day before from a preaching trip to a nearby village, and was catching up on paperwork and other practical details. And Mor tended the sick who came to the clinic. They ate lunch and took a short nap. Then as they were getting ready for afternoon coffee, at about 2:30, they heard the unpleasant thunder of bombers in the air. Far ran out into the yard to look and came right back. It looked like thirty to forty planes in the air, more than he had ever seen before in Hequ.

"We must stay where we are," he told Mor. "There is no time to run for shelter. Quickly, let's get under the bed."

Before he got properly under the bed, and while Mor had just bent down to get under, they heard the sound of the first bomb exploding. It was a sharper sound than they had heard in previous air raids. Deafening noises seemed to be coming at them from every direction. The crisis lasted only a few minutes. Mor was deafened by the sound, and finding it difficult to open her eyes for the smoke. But by barely squinting, while still dazed, she knew instinctively the walls had fallen on her husband.

Somehow Mor, who was small and light, had been picked up by the wind rushing out from the explosion, and thrown by the blast onto a pile of stones, broken glass and splinters of wood. For a brief moment she heard the cry of her husband before he was completely buried under the ruins of our home.

She could not understand how she could be alive, when a moment before she thought her last minute on earth had come. There were flames around her when she first rose to her feet. There she stood— alone and helpless with the dearest person on earth lost under the debris. Most of the Chinese around had made it to a shelter, except for five women with bound feet who could not run.

The air was heavy and black, and filled with the cries of the wounded. Suddenly Chinese friends from the church and young businessmen came running to Mor's aid, even though most of them had also homes buried in ruins. It took them half an hour to dig out their pastor from the rubble.

Lao Quan, who was part of Mor and Far's staff, remembers that Mor was crying and shouting when he arrived from the bomb shelter at the church. He told us Far was hit by the center beam of the house, which fell on the bed under which he was hiding. The mud-brick walls fell easily. When they dug him out from under the ruins Mor pleaded, "Be careful of his head."

But there was no breath in him. The fallen beam had struck his head. Quan told us he embraced his pastor under the quilt that covered him. ("Seven days we prayed hoping he would come alive," Quan added.)

As a nurse, Mor looked at Far and knew that there was not much hope, but she tried artificial respiration. After two hours there was still no sign of life. Then she relaxed for a moment and looked around for a place for Far to lie. As she stood there in the bitter December cold, with her home like a gaping wound open to the street, all in chaos and covered with dirt, she couldn't even find a decent place to lay her beloved.

It seemed like something had been blasted inside as well as outside herself. Her world was falling apart from within and without. For one brief moment she wondered if she were losing her mind or if this was all just a bad dream. In the next moment, she wished she were with

Far in that "land that is fairer than day," instead of in a world that was blown apart. Here in the sanctuary of her home everything had changed.

In the midst of her despair, Mor and her circle of faithful friends continued to hover around Far into the twilight hours. They talked and wept together. Then suddenly one of the Chinese friends reported that there was looting going on in the other rooms that were also blown open to the street.

Mor couldn't believe it. While none of those who were robbing her were people she knew, she had never expected any resident of Hequ to steal from her in her hour of sorrow. Later she saw the situation more clearly in the light of the terrible poverty people lived in. But right then, this was a final hammer blow that further shattered her hopes.

Still not wanting to believe that her dear Peter was really dead, she suddenly heard the voice of the Almighty, "You do not realize now what I am doing, but later you will understand" (Jn 13:7). That's the only time in her life she heard the audible voice of God, and she was comforted.

She also remembered the voice of her dear husband again as she noticed that the calendar was still hanging among the ruins, with the message Far had accepted and shared with her just a few hours earlier. She returned and read alone the words she had read hand-in-hand with Peter that very morning after breakfast: "As the heavens are higher than the earth, so are my ways higher than your ways." She didn't understand, but she accepted God's ways as higher than hers.

Then she looked at her beloved husband again, and the peaceful expression on his face. There wasn't a scar or wound of any sort. He looked as if he had just gone quickly into the presence of the Lord he had served. Her mind raced back over their years together. Suddenly she had a moment of truth, though she still could not comprehend it all. Yes, Peter Torjesen had kept the promise he made to God as a young man when he signed his life away with the words "And my life." He had been true to his word. He had given his life that others might live.

Life
Goes On

8

When dawn came to Hequ the next morning, Mor was still in shock. Into the night, she was relieved that there were practical details to be taken care of. These kept her going. First she started looking through the rubble for material to wash Far and prepare him for his grave. As she heard the dying still moaning outside her own ruined home, she was again grateful that Peter had gone quickly with no sign of pain.

She wrote in a letter four days later:

When at midnight he lay there dressed and ready, he looked so beautiful and peaceful— actually with a smile on his face. Our faithful co-workers Evangelist Nieh and Gatekeeper Wang, who had been at my side all the time and helped, then sat down and just wept. In this way we sat for a long time. They had to get it all out—

and we wept together, all three of us.

It has made a deep impression on them all that Peter had to lay down his life in this way, and 'die for us'—as they say. So they are given to tears all of them, both the workers and the congregation. I am constantly seeing new proofs of how they have become bonded to their foreign friend, the missionary, and how much they loved him. . . . I am so thankful to God that I was able to be here in Hequ at this time and stand at my dear husband's side—so this did not happen when Peter was here alone.

Tante Thora Arrives

Immediately a message was sent to Thora Johansen, their coworker in Hsuin Chen, where she had been ministering for six weeks. Far had recently been there with her and just returned to Hequ the day before the bombing. And now her Chinese Christian brothers came to tell her he was gone. Grief-stricken, they started the four-hour walk in the dark, with only an oil lamp to light their path. The little party of pilgrims reached Hequ at 2 a.m. Mor was relieved to see her faithful friend of many years. Again there was weeping. Thora reported that Peter had talked about heaven in his last sermon in Hsuin Chen. But his main thrust, as he addressed a crowd of several hundred in the marketplace, was the cross. He preached standing on a little mound, holding a large picture of the cross. He seemed to feel the needs of the crowd more than ever as he said to the people he loved, "Save your life while there is time." There wasn't much night left by the time Mor and Tante Thora found a place to sleep in the room that was least in shambles apart. Meanwhile Far's body didn't take long to freeze in the next room—among the ruins of his earthly home. So there was no need of embalming as they waited for colleagues to come to the funeral.

"Your mother was in shock for several days," Tante Thora told me later. Because of the continued bombing of Hequ, the two women found a place to rent that was attached to the Great Wall, the strongest shelter available. They spent their daytime hours at the edge of town, where bombs were less likely to fall. The days and nights were cold, and there was no coal to buy among the poor during wartime. So, Tante Thora said, they would tie chunks of coal to two ends of a rope, and thus carry as much coal as they could dangle over their shoulders back to their new place of refuge.

While the city was still suffering from the 250 to 300 bombs dropped on the tragic December 14, in the days following 60 bombs were dropped each day. But Mor had great confidence that God would spare her life, both for the sake of her children and for the comfort of her friends in Hequ.

The immediate problem was finding a burial place. Mor wrote about the incongruity of not being able to find a gravesite in a city she and Far had called home for so long:

We have never owned property here in Hequ, but lived in a rented house, like pilgrims, and now I can't find a resting place for my dear husband. We really experience that we are strangers and foreigners as day after day we have walked for miles out in the hills among the burial places. But nobody will sell one to us. After almost twenty years, to have lived and worked among these people, and finally to have laid down his life here, as Peter has, it seemed strange that it should be like this.

But in some ways Mor realized this was not so strange. To the pagan Chinese of that time, the grave was not only the place where the body of the dead was buried, but also the place where the spirit of the departed one was to be worshiped. As one CIM veteran of that time wrote,

At least twice yearly, food and drink are offered in worship at the graves of ancestors, and their spirits are supposed to come and

119

partake of the 'spiritual essence' of the offerings. Likewise, piles of imitation paper money, paper clothes, houses, sedan chairs, and other essentials which might be useful in the spirit world are burned at the graves, and are supposed to be thus transferred to the abode of the spirits for the use of the dead.

So it was fear of disturbing the spirits of their ancestors that kept people from giving Far a grave on their property. Knowing about this and the ancestor worship that would take place at the surrounding graves if Far were buried in a usual burial place, Mor was most happy when God had a Joseph of Arimathea (Mt 27:57-60) in the wings to give Far a resting place. This godly man came and offered Mor a beautiful burial lot on his farm.

Mor was also able to write home before the funeral about the general response among people to Far's tragic death:

God is speaking in a powerful way to people in this city through what has happened, we feel. If God saw that such a big sacrifice had to be made in order that people would accept the Good News of the Cross—which Peter till his last day before his departure preached—then I and our dear children also have to be willing to give this offering.

Far's message of the unconditional love of God for us, evidenced on the cross, continued to speak to people in utter despair. For not only Far had been killed on December 14, but several hundred other residents of Hequ. And the wounded that day were too numerous to count. With the dead and the wounded and most of the city of mudbrick dwellings in ruins, Hequ has never recovered from the devastation. Imagine the suffering in a city with no emergency hospital or Red Cross unit, no disaster relief, and no social services of any kind. But there was one place people could still go for comfort and help. And as they realized the price Mor and Far had paid to stay with them through the ravages of war, they were more open than ever to their message of God's love coming to us in Jesus Christ.

Arrivals for the Funeral

Fourteen days after Far died, two of his good friends from the mission arrived by horseback: Sverre Holth after a four-days' journey, and Georg Rinvold after two days of travel. Onkel Sverre describes what they found:

> What a sight met us in Hequ. House after house lay in ruins, and here and there lay mutilated corpses that still were not buried after the terrible bombing. . . . A pile of stones and earth marked the place that had once been the Torjesens' bedroom and where his dear wife and co-workers had dug him out that frightening afternoon. . . . We were not too late as the burial place was just found the day before.
>
> . . . A small group of eager believers—young men—were busy with the funeral preparations. Because there was no church building [it lay in ruins], a large tent was set up and beautifully decorated inside and out. Hands of love had woven memory wreaths from artificial flowers, and banners with moving words . . . were sent from near and far. The memorial service was held Sunday afternoon, December 31. . . . There were many hundreds attending with more outside the tent than there was room for inside.

Over the entrance to the tent hung a silk banner which read, "He gave his life to save the people," while in the middle of the white tent (the Chinese color for mourning) sat the casket covered with a Chinese and a Norwegian flag. Also the messages of love given to Far by church members and townspeople were in white. But the German Catholic priest brought his banner in black silk. Mor writes, "When the various ones got up to give a last greeting, the priest stood up and spoke about 'Greater love has no man than this that he lay down his life for his friends.' It was very good. . . . The thread that ran through the whole celebration was that he gave his life to save the people of this place. That spoke its powerful message more than any sermon. How bonded our Chinese friends were to Peter and how they loved him."

The Burial at Dawn

Because of the possibility of air raids, the burial took place early the next morning, January 1, 1940. But first Mor writes about the most memorable New Year's Eve of her life:

> All night a group of young men watched over the casket. Sitting around an open fire before the tent, they sang praises to God's honor, so all living around there could hear their songs of thanks for their Savior, and for the one who had brought them the message. What a testimony for the pagans who knew these were not just words. They had seen living proof that Christians took trials differently. They had a God of comfort to go to. We do not sorrow as those who have no hope.
>
> Next morning people arrived early. Many of the women had not gone home, but sat up all night. . . . It took 45 minutes for the quiet procession to make its way at dawn—on the first day of the year. . . . In a peaceful place named "Water and Grass Valley" our dear father and husband was laid to rest in China's yellow soil, where he will remain till the resurrection morning. What a glorious hope for all who are sorrowing. We shall meet again.

Onkel Sverre also added to the story of the burial in his article for the mission paper, *Kinamisjonaeren:* "Both under the worship time before the casket was taken out and during the ceremony at the grave, an impressive stillness—after Chinese standards—reigned. Not much was said. Hearts were too full. Eighteen young strong Christian men carried their pastor to his last resting place, while just as many walked in front of the casket with banners. One of these read, "A good shepherd has died for me." A large group of mourning friends walked behind the casket. The burial place is about 2 kilometers from town."

The Theme of the Cross
Tante Thora picked up the theme of the cross as she wrote home to Norway. She said that Peter Torjesen

> always, whether he was home or out, lifted high the banner of the Cross. On the street, in the church, or out in the villages, he wanted the Cross to bring the light. . . . I thought it was such a mighty testimony [that] on top of the casket stood the red Cross decorated with paper flowers in all colors (there are no real flowers here in winter)—highlighted by the morning sunlight. It made me think of the song, "The Cross Lights the Path All the Way."

She goes on to say that in these almost twenty years in Hequ, Far had climbed every hill and valley. And he could "eat bitterness," the Chinese would say about him. What they meant was that he would willingly "eat" the bitterness others were "eating" around him, sharing their sorrow and empathizing with them. Thora continues,

> He never spared himself to bring the happy message of the Cross to the most hidden or forgotten village. His wish was that "The Cross will be seen where the idol once stood." May God bless and strengthen his wife and children who are left without a dear husband and father. The children wrote in one of the last letters to Mor and Far—which he never read because he was already home with Jesus—"It is for Jesus' sake that we are separated."

That's why the banner from us children at the funeral read, "The last greeting to our dear Far with thanks for all you have meant to us," and then in large print, "IT WAS FOR JESUS' SAKE."

We Children Hear the News
Meanwhile, miles away in Chefoo, we received the telegram informing us that Far had been killed, but Mor was safe. It had taken ten days

to reach us through the war zones.

The principal called me to her office, and in as kindly a way as she knew how, gave me the news. Life came to a complete halt. One of my favorite teachers told me years later, "You looked as if all joy had gone out of your heart."

Edvard had already been called to the Teachers' Lounge by "Mr. Bee" (a nickname) and shown the telegram. Mr. Bee didn't know what to say, so shared, "Peace I leave with you. . . . I do not give to you as the world gives. Do not let your hearts be troubled. . . ." Then they knelt in prayer. "The world collapsed," Ed said later, "but John 14:27 sustained all of us during those days, and Mr. Bee with a minimum of words helped."

Hakon was touched by a teacher arranging supper for him in her dining room. He also had a sense of despair, but the immediate problem was that all the boys he was living with were too nice to him. He was not being teased and treated like a human being among the hundred boys in the dorm, where each often looked out for himself.

When Torje was called to the principal's office, he was afraid he had broken another rule. Last time he had been called he had been strapped. But now he was given a cup of tea before being told the news. Like Hakon, he also found it a depressing experience when later everyone, out of concern for his loss, was passing him the food at the table. Usually nobody thought of passing any food to anyone else.

Later we four children were together. Torje remembered, "Edvard gave a lot of security to us." Edvard seemed to instinctively feel that he had to take on the father role, and was concerned about our individual welfare. He was willing to talk and let us ask questions, as we knew so little about what had happened. We wondered why the Japanese would bomb our house when Norway was a neutral nation, and we asked why there was no bomb shelter. It all seemed incredible.

I later wrote to my grandmother, "Torje took it so sweetly. After

124

he had just heard the news, I began to read about heaven to him, and reminded him we would see Far in heaven. But he started telling me right away that he had led two boys to say 'Yes' to Jesus whom he had been together with at the hospital when he had diphtheria." He was glad they would be in heaven too, with Far and the rest of us.

That time in the hospital had been a special time when God had been preparing both Torje and me for what was coming. Because Torje had diphtheria, and I had been with him just before he got sick, I too was quarantined. There Torje had much to share about his talks with God while he was sick, how he prayed for Mor and Far, as well as his friends who didn't know Jesus.

Even as an eight-year-old, Torje seemed to be able to discern that our folks needed our prayers. I also had the sense that they were in danger. In the hospital I had a dream in which they were struggling for their lives. As I worried and prayed about it, God gave me a tremendous peace that he would take care of it all.

When Edvard was asked by some of the teachers how we were able to take the news of our father's death so bravely, he answered, "The Lord had already shown us that we would not see our father again." Here he was referring to the sense both he and I had after we had said goodbye to Mor and Far, the feeling that our family life would not be the same again. To Edvard it was clearer than to me that we would not see Far again. This sense cushioned us against the shock when it did happen. Far's death was not a total surprise to any of us.

"Adapting to Far's death took the pressure off adapting to Chefoo," one of my brothers later remarked. "The language issue got lost—and we learned the language by thinking of and trying to express this bigger tragedy in English."

This was especially true of Hakon who, immediately after Far's death, founded the *Children's Monthly Paper*. It is remarkable that after three months as a Norwegian student in an English-speaking school, he was brave enough to become the editor of a fledging newspaper. The purpose of the paper was to raise funds for the Jews who had to escape from Hitler in Europe, and were pouring into Shanghai. Because of this new need in Shanghai, some CIM missionaries were loaned from work with Chinese to work with Jews.

In the newspaper Hakon learned to express the tragedy of Far's death in his new language. He wrote:

Before it happened I was really warned. How I do not know, but I know it was God who did it. He was only testing me to see if I really believed in him and understood that he had taken my father to himself. . . . Before my parents left me I knew that I was not going to see my father any more though I did not realize it then, just like the disciples did not realize that Jesus was going to suffer on the cross.

Later I overheard one of Hakon's classmates read this piece aloud. As an eleven-year-old she did not know how to react, except to giggle and trivialize the tragedy with, "Oh, listen to Hakon Torjesen describe his father's death." Another girl joined her in laughing over what he had written.

Hearing this, I rushed for the outhouse, the only place of privacy in the boarding school. There I sobbed my heart out.

But God also had his comforters in place. During the long winter holidays there were special meetings for those of us who could not go home for Christmas. That January, the leaders were Alice and James Taylor (James was the grandson of Hudson Taylor). In boarding school with us was their son, James Taylor III, now head of the Overseas Missionary Fellowship, formerly the CIM.

"The Second Coming of Jesus" was the theme of the special meetings. Still struggling with my sorrow, I was helped by the reminder that this world is not the end of life, but only the beginning. I drank in the beautiful description of Jesus' coming given us in 1 Thessalonians 4:13-18. It was now about Far, since he was among those "who have fallen asleep." Suddenly I saw the light; I needn't "grieve like the rest of men, who have no hope . . . [for] the dead in Christ will rise first. After that, we who are still alive and are left will be caught up together with them in the clouds to meet the Lord in the air." It was too good to be true. A passage I had never noticed before suddenly sounded as if God had "Taylor-made" it for me.

There were also many who wrote to us, both from Norway and China, to express their empathy in our grief. Sometimes I did not dare open these letters in front of others in case of another "waterfall." So I would take them to the blessed outhouse to read. On another occasion I was fighting the tears in the classroom during a music appreciation class. The song we were listening to on the old gramophone was a Scottish ballad to a fallen hero:

He's gone on the mountains,

He's gone on the prairies,

Like a summer-dried fountain

When our need was the sorest.

It came too close to how I felt about my fallen hero, Far. I felt as if I never needed a father more than I did just then.

Concern about Mor
We tended to seesaw between thinking of Far who was gone, and Mor who might be in danger of her life at the moment. One of our concerns was how soon would we see her. We were glad that she had found a safer place to stay (up against the more than 2,000-year-old Great Wall, with a dugout in the old wall for protection from bombs). Torje wrote to Mor, "I hope the new house is very nice. . . . I am so glad the bombers have not bombed this house. From your boy, Torje."

Like Nicodemus stealing to Jesus in the night, Communists came to this hiding place to see Mor, ask questions and express sympathy and appreciation that her husband had laid down his life for China. When she showed them the family picture with Far and us four children, many of them had tears in their eyes. They were open and willing to hear her tell the story of Jesus coming to save us all. Some of them confessed that up to this time they thought people would only die for Communism, but now they had seen another side to life. As Mor wrote about such opportunities, we understood why she stayed. And yet we worried for her safety.

The Shock of War in Norway

That April, Germany invaded Norway. One more point of Mor's security system was gone. She wrote to her mother, "It was a shock for me to receive the news of the war in Norway. Right after all that I have lost, it is as if dear Norway is gone too now. But again it is good to remember that we are only pilgrims here on earth. Our citizenship is in heaven. From there we are waiting for our Savior, Jesus Christ."

I also wrote to my grandmother, "How terrible that Norway is also in the war zone. I can't believe it. As we have been in the war here, and hear about the war in Europe, I've always thought of Norway as one peaceful place left in the world."

Mor was happy to receive a personal letter from General He Lung, a famous Communist general, expressing his sympathy that Norway had been invaded by the Germans. This contact with He Lung helped restore order in the Hequ area, after the Japanese through their persistent bombing had broken the age-old rural police power system that had kept the landed gentry and urban property owners in control for centuries. Into this vacuum came He Lung's army. The Reds in this case cooperated with the Nationalist government against the Japanese.

Mor writes about these new faces around town:

We have had no trouble with them. . . . They get very quiet and tender some times when they have arrived a bit proud and hard.

. . . When they see Peter's picture, they say quietly to each other that he gave his life in this place. Then it is as if one can feel the fear of God coming over these so often godless people. Then they look at the children's picture and they think it is very fortunate to have three sons and one daughter. And then they become so friendly, and assure us they are coming again! So we thank God that he can bend the hearts like a stream of water. Several of them have also listened intently at our meetings.

A New Church Building

By May 1940 things were also looking brighter for the church. The congregation had bought a new place to meet. Tante Thora and Mor reported:

What God has allowed to happen has made a deep impression on them. The church and mission that had been their "home" was destroyed, and their . . . shepherd God took home. But the congregation was still there. That the "birds" from the air could not destroy, and they felt the responsibility as never before. . . . Soon the money began to come in and such a willingness to give we have never seen in Hequ before. . . . In May the contract was signed. . . . It was a happy day for all of us. There is room for church, school, street chapel, and reception rooms for men and women.

This was the group of believers who had been told by the pagans in Hequ after the bombing, "Now that your church is in ruins and your pastor dead, this must be the end of the Christian church in Hequ." This was not said with scorn, but with a sense of fatalism.

"Oh, no," two of the leading Christian businessmen had said, "We are all here, and we are the church."

It was these dedicated Christians who wrote to us children the most beautiful letter from all the members of the Hequ congregation, sharing our sorrow:

129

Dearest four children! Remember that we in full measure and with the deepest feelings are with you in your sorrow over your greatly loved father who has left you. How much we want to share this deep sadness and sorrow with you. But though we cannot take a part of the sorrow away from you, we can help by praying for you. And we believe that through this you will receive great comfort and strength. For God who each day carries our burdens will comfort you, so the sorrow will not be too much for you.

Mor Journeys to See Us

At last, Mor had written home to the mission, "I think the pillar of cloud is beginning to move. We have not felt this way before, but rather that we [she and Thora] should not leave the congregation as sheep without a shepherd, and without a place for them to gather."

But now there was a new church building, and Mor was encouraged by the Christian maturity she saw in the Hequ congregation. And so with her shepherd's heart at peace, she started preparing for the long journey to the coast to see us children. First she had to go northwest through the Ordos Desert for eight days by cart to Baotou, before going southeast to Chefoo by train and ship. Shorter routes were closed. Old Mr. Shuen, age 80, offered to accompany her. "I have had a good rich life," he told her, "And now I want to do one more service for my Lord before I die, and that is to help you reach your children. If I never make it back to Hequ, I'm in God's hands."

As Torje heard about the hazardous journey, he wrote, "I hope you have a nice time, dear Mother, and no robbers will kill you, dear Mother. God be with you on the journey so you will not fall." After big brother Edvard had talked to Torje, Edvard wrote to Mor, "He's so excited about your coming and has prayed all day for you."

As we heard about the trip after she finally arrived, it proved that Mor needed both Torje's and everyone else's prayers. The first crisis was just before crossing the Yellow River from the Chinese side to the Japanese side. There were frightening robbers in the area. But then a high-ranking Chinese officer spoke kindly to Mor from atop his horse, "Don't you know me from Sunday school?" God had sent him just in time to escort them past the danger.

At the river, there were many Chinese waiting to cross. Because Mor and Mr. Shuen lacked a Japanese pass they were told they could not go. But suddenly someone in the crowd, probably a sympathetic Chinese, produced a pass. Everyone in the crowd looked so happy when she and Mr. Shuen got on the ferry. On the other side of the river the real adventure started.

In the Ordos desert most people had never seen a foreign woman before, so Mor was quite a curiosity—a small and skinny White woman on a cart with the ancient Mr. Shuen. The second night they came to an inn where three travelers had been killed at dawn. The third day they were met by a military company rushing toward them with weapons. Probably the soldiers were disarmed by the sight of utter weakness in the little woman and the old man. Or maybe the pair had the protection of angelic hosts, and so was not attacked. The fourth night they came to a Mongolian inn with all kinds of guests, including thirty opium smokers with whom they had to share the bedroom. "Mr. Shuen was quiet in prayer to God," wrote Mor. "Without God everything could have gone wrong."

At a later point, when they crossed from the Japanese side to where the Reds were in charge, Mor was taken prisoner for a day. She marched in the heat of the June sun with no food or water. She told us of the problem of going to the bathroom with what seemed like a whole regiment of soldiers around her. When she asked for permission to go off the road to urinate, she was commanded just to squat where she was and do it. But of course she was too nervous to produce. Finally one of the officers sounded very worldly-wise as he told the rest, "These foreigners are strange. They can't just do it like we do, so we'll have to leave." What he forgot to mention was that she was not just a foreigner, but a lone, unprotected woman among a herd of soldiers.

After a whole day as a prisoner, she and her captors came to Japanese-occupied territory, where everyone either had to hide or show their credentials. When Mor showed hers, a Japanese general came to her aid. She told him of her husband's death and her desire to see her four children. He gave her a pass and saw that she got on her way. Thus with all the delays of war, it took her three weeks to reach us by cart, ferry, foot, train and ship.

The four of us were jumping with joy that summer day as the ship glided slowly toward the pier in Chefoo. Way up on the top deck we spotted Mor's smiling face. Suddenly I realized her brown hair had turned gray since September. That said much about what she had suffered since I saw her. But by the time she came down the gangplank, I was too excited about being with her again to think of her having changed. Suddenly, we were all lost in hugs and kisses.

We got a little apartment for the one-month summer holidays. The talking and catching up on everything was interspersed with trips to the beach. It was interesting to see Edvard taking Far's place, sharing the concerns of the family with Mor. For instance, the apartment needed to be furnished, so there was some buying, and even more borrowing, of furniture that needed to be done. I was so glad for Mor when Edvard took charge and got things done.

It was too good to be true to be together again and ask all the questions we had hidden inside ourselves since Far's death. Of course there were many painful moments when we all relived the whole tragedy. And there were tears, open tears that washed away the inner pain of having tried to keep things to ourselves and not burden others with our grief. Now we were alone as a family and could let it all out.

But in all the long talks we had about it all, there was never any hint of doubting or questioning God why Far had to leave us. It had been a costly but a good year. Our close Hequ friend Ragnhild Syvertsen, who had spoken at Far's memorial service in Oslo, summarized our feelings as we read her speech: "Costly in the sight of the Lord is the death of the godly. This does not mean God does not put a high value on his children's lives. But precisely because they are so precious to him, therefore their death also becomes very costly."

And so with our hearts at peace, we enjoyed a summer of long and relaxed mealtimes, and whole mornings and afternoons of swimming or taking long walks along the beach. Edvard took charge of the canoe, which Far had bought us the summer before, and supervised us as we each had our turn to set out to sea. Mor wrote home to her mother that just being with us in such a lovely setting had rejuvenated her.

As September drew close we knew we had to go back to school. What we dreaded most was having Mor return to Hequ. I admired her for her willingness, but secretly wished God would close the door so she wouldn't have to take the long, hazardous journey back again. With all the uncertainty of the war escalating in Europe, and rumors of further Japanese aggression in Asia, everyone around us remained in suspense. There was a sense of foreboding as we listened to Mor talking with her CIM colleagues.

Pearl Harbor
and
Prison Camp

9

After the summer Mor left us for Beijing, to try at least to get back to her home province (Shanxi), even though she knew the way to Hequ was temporarily closed. She wrote to her mother that September, "How good it will be when we are finally home in heaven . . . no more traveling. . . . No more separation. At the same time, I wouldn't change with anyone, but thank and praise God that I am well enough to return to Shanxi and the ministry again."

Beijing was full of Shanxi missionaries, waiting for passes to return to their posts. To their surprise, Mor and two other Scandinavians got their passes and train tickets after just a couple of days in Beijing, and were ready to go to Shanxi the next day. But suddenly the political situation between the Japanese and the Allied nations became so tense their trip was canceled. So Mor took care of Tante Signe (see chapter 1), who had been ill. The Salvation Army kindly lent all the stranded Norwegian missionaries a house, free of charge. This was especially helpful since no money could be sent out of Norway after Hitler's invasion.

Before Christmas it was evident that no missionaries could return to Shanxi. The fighting there was heavy, the lines were closed and the Japanese in Beijing refused passes to all the missionaries. The Norwegians no longer enjoyed the privilege of being neutral, because after the German invasion of Norway, King Hakon escaped to London and set up his Norwegian government in exile, a government that included armed forces fighting with the Allies.

With no other open door before her, Mor came back to Chefoo. We were overjoyed and had a marvelous Christmas together. But first we remembered December 14, the day Far died, and thanked God for all the ways we had been cared for by our heavenly father during this first year without Far. One of the most moving letters we got, commemorating the first anniversary of Far's death, was from the Catholic priest in Hequ who wrote with great sensitivity to all of us. (See Appendix 2.)

After the Christmas holidays, we returned to boarding school and Mor stayed at the CIM guest house, wondering what her next move should be. But in spite of this uncertainty, she was so grateful that in the midst of all the upheaval in China, we were safe. She wrote to her mother,

> Peter was so determined that if we had any control over the situation, we should not put the children through terrible situations because we are missionaries. And it is all of grace that God has taken such care of our children. The fact that they offered their father for Jesus' sake has not made them bitter or hard, but only driven them more than ever to follow Jesus and live for him. . . .

God has also used them to be a blessing to others at the school.

A Ministry for Mor

In March 1941, God also opened a new ministry for Mor in Chefoo. The mission home, with room for forty guests, needed a new hostess, and she was invited to take the post. It was a perfect situation, giving her a designated way of contributing to the community, as well as taking care of her need for support for her family. God had provided miraculously from month to month since money from Norway was stopped. But now her support was officially coming from a new source. Mor was thankful.

While we children lived in the dorm at school, we were just five minutes' walk from Mor, and could come home for a visit each afternoon and go home to her on weekends and holidays. That spring and summer we again enjoyed family life. We all four agreed that dorm life was fun, but we also agreed that being separated from our parents was no fun. This way we got the best of both worlds.

Evening walks on the beautiful beach offered opportunities for Mor to share her heart with Edvard. She wanted to tell him about Far's concern for the Mongols—how in the last years he had talked much about leaving the Chinese work when it was established, and pioneering across the Yellow River from Hequ among the Mongols. Edvard picked up the challenge and believed God had called him to continue Far's work. He caught the vision of reaching the Mongols, who had never heard the gospel.

But if Edvard was to follow in Far's footsteps he obviously needed some training. Where could he go? This problem lay heavily on Mor for months before Edvard graduated. Before Germany invaded Norway, the plan had been for us kids to go back to Norway for our college educations. But now that door was closed. And while Far had been in the United States, and Mor knew some of his friends through

137

letters, she did not feel she could ask any of them to take in Edvard.

But again God had laid it on the heart of one of his servants, Torrey Mosvold, to help us. Mor had met him in Norway before he moved to Brooklyn, New York. When Torrey read in the *New York Herald* that Peter Torjesen had been killed by a bomb—the first missionary to die in the war against China—he was deeply concerned. When four months later Germany invaded Norway, he knew that meant none of the Torjesens could go back home. One day he felt compelled by the "inner voice" to write Mor and offer his help. The day after he mailed his letter, he got one from Mor. She had heard the same "inner voice." And so God had a home prepared to receive Edvard in the new world of the United States.

We all dreaded another breakup in the family when Edvard would leave us that August 1941. It was hard for Mor not only to lose him, but to send him to the U.S., which was unknown to her. We children were losing a big brother who had begun to take Far's place among us. Often we younger ones told him our problems when we didn't want Mor to have any more to worry about. We all had great confidence in his judgment.

But we were grateful he could go. Later we were also grateful for the job he got with the Norwegian Government Service, as landing agent for all Norwegian ships coming into New York harbor. With a large merchant marine fleet, Norway contributed to the war in this way. And for Edvard this job was recognized in lieu of military service, required of all young Norwegians outside Norway. After all we had seen of the horrors of war, we were glad Edvard did not have to go into combat.

Pearl Harbor

When Pearl Harbor was bombed four months later, we were even more grateful that Edvard had left on the last ship from China. For suddenly we were all prisoners, under house arrest. Guards were at our gate with a notice posted, reading, "These premises are under the control of Great Japan's Navy." The city of Chefoo had been under Japanese rule since 1938 when the governor of Shandong Province had made a pact with the enemy, so we were used to the sight of Japanese guards on duty—with their steel helmets, khaki uniforms, heavy boots and bayonets. But this was different. On December 8, 1941 (Asian time), Japan had declared war on Britain and America.

It was yet another in a series of shocks over the past four years: first the invasion of peaceful Hequ by Japan, then Far's death, followed by Germany's invasion of Norway. Now suddenly the whole world was thrown in the big boiling pot of violence and destruction. Part of the shock was to discover that the same Japanese who in Chefoo had treated us with an almost-casual indifference, as aliens among their enemies, were now treating us as the real enemies. We all had to wear armbands to identify our nationalities when we left the compound, as well as carry with us our record of vaccinations. The Japanese would ask us gruffly for these, and mercilessly scold us if we were not complying with the rules.

It was easy to let our imaginations run away with us and visualize the worst that could happen. Edvard's good friend Norman Cliff did just that when he later wrote in the *The Courtyard of the Happy Way,* "We pictured ourselves being transported to Japan and doing hard labor; and what if the Allies lost the war? Would we be prisoners for life? The rationing of food too had its effect. We were growing boys and found ourselves perpetually hungry."

Prison Camp

By the summer of 1942 Japanese officials warned us that we might soon be evacuated to South Africa. Our school compound was needed for Great Japan's Army. Other rumors had us moving to Shanghai or Manchuria. Slowly the Japanese started taking over one building at a time. Then came the orders we had five days to move out—200 children, staff and retired workers. As we packed, scores of Japanese soldiers surrounded us, putting tags on everything they wanted. Anyone who had a radio, a camera, a watch or a nice set of china lost it. It was infuriating to watch them put stickers on each thing of value around us to tell us that this piece of property now belongs to the Japanese forces.

But there was not much time to vent our anger. Our new bosses wanted us off the CIM compound as soon as possible. We all felt helpless with our captors shouting at us to hurry. And so each person was allowed one small trunk and bedding as we mournfully left the school for prison on November 5, 1942. Later we would often sing of the school:

For we love that old school by the old China shore,

And we'll sing its praises o'er and o'er,

But the Chefoo school shall be no more

By the side of the sea at Chefoo.

During the months of uncertainty one of the teachers had composed this song. Hudson Taylor had chosen the lovely spot by the sea for a school for missionaries' children back in 1881. Many memories passed through the minds of adults and some older students as we left the compound, some in rickshaws but most of us walking. For many the greater concern, however, was where were we going. For how long? And would we starve?

Then such morose thoughts were interrupted by another song:

God is still on the throne, and He will remember His own.

Though trials may press us and burdens distress us,

He never will leave us alone.

God is still on the throne, and He will remember His own.

His promise is true, He will not forget you,

God is still on the throne.

Children and adults gradually all joined in and, as someone later wrote, "the many Chinese onlookers were . . . wide-eyed. The foreign devils' God seemed to help them in adversity." On the last lap of the journey, as we climbed up Temple Hill, we sang, "God is our refuge" (based on Psalm 46). Finally we reached the prison, four missionary houses of the American Presbyterian Mission. A fifth house was already occupied by the business community.

The four CIM houses continued to be run as extensions of the four large buildings on the campus we had just left. The four units that were transferred to the prison camp were the boys' dormitory, the girls' dormitory, the prep-school dormitory for boys and girls, grades one to four, and the guest house. In each house those who had been in charge before continued to be so. Thus Mor carried on as the head of the fourth house.

I wrote in my journal,

What a queer place! And how everyone was running in and out on top of each other, and no one knowing how 47 people were to get into an eight-room house. But soon people knew at least where to dump their stuff. Picnic lunch was served in the kitchen in the midst of it all. Mor arrived late with the other big shots. . . . Never shall I forget the whole assembly settling down on the staircase, on boxes in that narrow hall and having supper.

And later,

Peggy, Trix, Grace and I got chucked in the small verandah porch about 10' by 5'. . . like an icebox in winter, reaching 26 degrees F when we got up. And yet what fun we had. . . .

Of course, there were still rumors of where we might go—put into verse and sung to the tune of "The British Grenadiers,"

Some talk of 'vacuation, and some, I'm also told,
Of hostile transportation to Peking's temples old.

But whatever information may reach this distant hill,
We're here in concentration, and bright and happy still.

Some talk of far Lourenco, and some of bare Cathay,
And some of Shanghai's compounds, so we didn't know what to say.
But of all the world's great places, there's nowhere with such thrill
As living in small spaces in Chefoo's Temple Hill.

Weihsien Civil Assembly Centre

But before anything as exotic as moving to Lourenco Marques in
Mozambique could materialize, we heard in August of 1943 that we
were to transfer to Weihsien Civil Assembly Centre. We weren't even
leaving Shandong Province, but merely going two days by ship to
Qingdao, 130 miles by train to Weifang and then by truck to Weihsien.
There we would became part of a larger prison camp of 1,600 prisoners who stayed together until the end of World War 2.

I vividly remember the two nights in the hold of the ship. That part
of the ship was meant for freight, not humans, so it had neither been
cleaned nor aired for years. A foul stench of mixed odors met us as
we entered. Since there was hardly room to move, we all lay down,
with our bodies squashed next to each other. And then the cock-
roaches started to crawl over us, too many to catch or kill. As about
250 of us lay there, with a curtain dividing the girls from the boys,
suddenly a little girl started crying with fright from the darkness and
strange smells. Others began to feel seasick as the ship rolled in the
choppy water. Norman Cliff wrote, "The floor was hard, the ship was
rocking, our stomachs were hungry and rats were running over us. As
I dozed off into a light sleep I could hear the girls a few yards away
on the other side of the 'curtain' singing in harmony:

Jesus, Savior, pilot me
Over life's tempestuous sea;

142

Unknown waves before me roll,

Hiding rock and treacherous shoal;

Chart and compass come from Thee;

Jesus, Savior, pilot me.

After the journey at sea followed seven hours by train, with no water and lots of dust. It was a dry September day and the fields around us had been scorched by the summer sun. Along with the heat came the difficult and frightening question that stuck between our parched lips: "Where are we really going? And are things going to continue to get worse at each stage?"

Mor wrote, "The trip was unforgettable. We felt what it was to be prisoners." And a friend, David Michell, wrote in *A Boy's War,*

A lot of our baggage was lost or broken into en route. . . . We were only given two minutes to get everything off the train. . . . As we dusted off ourselves and our belongings, half-dazed from the abrupt exodus, we heard shouts from hustling guards, telling us to climb into the waiting open trucks and a few ramshackle buses. . . . After a mile or two high walls and fortified towers came into view . . . we saw Japanese sentries standing guard with fixed bayonets. . . . [A]nd two big wooden gates with an inscription in Chinese, THE COURTYARD OF THE HAPPY WAY. We had reached Weihsien Camp.

This had been a Presbyterian compound with church, seminary, school—and a hospital where celebrities like Pearl Buck and Henry Luce were born. But by 1943, the place had suffered from looting and neglect. One early arrival described it as "bare walls, bare floors, dim electric light, no running water, primitive latrines, open cesspools, a crude bakery, two houses with public showers, three huge public kitchens, a desecrated church and a dismantled hospital, a few sheds for shops, rows of cell-like rooms, and three high dormitories for persons who are single."

143

But when we arrived from Chefoo, about 350 weary travelers, this camp had been turned into an ordered community. "It runs like clockwork," Mor wrote to Edvard. "We all have our community duties. . . . For everything we do we stand in queues . . . many times a day." Indeed, there were lines to get our food, water, boiled water for drinking, coal dust (to mix with clay and water to make coal balls), and lines to the latrine. With 1,600 prisoners the lines were unavoidable. Yet the organization amazed us all. The committees had started functioning in March 1943 with the early arrivals.

One of these, Mary Scott, was the only woman on a committee. She wrote later in *Kept in Safeguard,*

> The Japanese . . . had worked out a plan of government for our "village." They requested that . . . chairmen and assistants for nine camp committees be selected: General Affairs, Discipline, Labor, Education, Supplies, Quarters, Medicine, Engineering, and Finance.

Besides this "white collar" job Mary worked in the kitchen:

> The same week I supervised the serving team, I was also latrine cleaner. It kept me hurrying all morning to complete the latrine cleanup, take a shower . . . and get to the kitchen in time.

In her spare time she coached boys, including Torje, at baseball.

> My "boys" invited me to tea one afternoon. Seven signed their names. . . . I still have this invitation, written in pencil, among my treasured souvenirs.

Olympic Hero Eric Liddell

Another hero who spent all his spare time with the younger set was Eric Liddell of *Chariots of Fire* fame. He had created a world record when he won the 400-meter race for Britain in the 1924 Olympics, after first having refused to run on Sunday in the Games that year. Within a year of his international success, this "Flying Scotsman" left for

China as a missionary. In camp he planned the recreational activities for the young by day, and in the evening spent time with them playing chess, or just in quiet conversation. Perhaps more than any other person, the man we all called "Uncle Eric" brought hope to both the "mish kids" and the more secular crowd.

It has been said of him by a fellow prisoner that, in our little world that measured 150 by 200 yards, "he was without doubt the person most in demand and most respected and loved. . . ." Ours was a world in microcosm. There were twenty nationalities represented among the 1,600 prisoners, with businessmen, government officials, missionaries, prostitutes, junkies and assorted troublemakers that had enjoyed the freedom of being foreigners in China—far away from home. While we were not tortured as prisoners were in other camps, we received little food and lived with open cesspools, rats, flies and disease. Without the generous support of Christians like Liddell, many of these would never have been able to manage the rigors of life in a crowded prison camp. Liddell could be found putting up a wooden shelf for a former prostitute one day and carrying coal balls to an elderly person the next day.

One of my great moments in camp came when I was alone in a kitchen, singlehandedly trying to kill hundreds of flies before 600 people would file in for their rations. Then Eric Liddell was passing by. I knew him well, both as my softball coach and as a Bible teacher. Now he stopped in and gave me his undivided attention for a few charged moments. With his steel-blue, penetrating and laughing eyes and a disarming smile, he had my complete attention. He told me that as a Christian I was bringing people nearer Christ by doing something as simple as killing flies for them. I had heard him teach that we either repel people from Christ or bring them closer. Then he heartily thanked me for what I was doing just then, with no one but God to notice what I was doing, or to give me proper credit.

Next to my father, Eric Liddell was the most Christlike person I

145

have ever met. When I was expecting my first child, the boy's name I had picked out was Erik Peter—after my two heroes. (But since I didn't have a boy, I am thrilled that Hakon's firstborn carries the great name Erik Peter Torjesen.)

Waging a War of Our Own

So with Uncle Eric's encouragement, I kept on swatting flies, and later became head of a team in an organized anti-fly campaign. Meanwhile, the Japanese authorities started a competition to stamp out the rats that were overrunning the camp. Then there were mosquitoes buzzing about and giving us malaria. And the bedbugs in all our mattresses that feasted on us by night. Hakon counted 500 one morning in his bed. (For a while he was storing all his dead bedbugs in a bottle to bring back to civilization!) We poured boiling water on mattresses and furniture in a vain attempt to kill them. So we itched and scratched some more.

Elizabeth Hoyte Goldsmith, who was nine when she came to Weihsien, writes in *Can God Be Trusted?* about the "hundreds of tiny flatbodied red bedbugs. Quite unfairly, they seemed to be particularly fond of me. My legs and arms became a mass of bites." Elizabeth was among the 94 children who came to Weihsien without their parents. Hers were serving as missionaries 1,000 miles away. The teachers in the Chefoo school had the extra responsibility of parenting these 94 children, as well as continuing their education without adequate classrooms, labs, textbooks and paper. Many classes were held outside, with the ground as the blackboard. After the war, Elizabeth asked one of her ex-teachers what she remembered about camp life. Her reply was, "Every night in the summer, I'd go over to where you were fast asleep. You'd lie sprawled across your sheet, soaked with perspiration and wearing as little as possible. My job would be to pick off all the bedbugs I could find."

By the summer of 1944 prison life was taking its toll. Besides mental breakdowns, many suffered with typhoid, dysentery or malaria. At the same time the food supply became more and more limited to flour, which was made into noodles, dumplings, bread porridge, bread pudding and so forth. Interviewed by a Vancouver paper after the war, one couple said our diet for two years consisted of "leeks, poor quality vegetables, a very little poor meat and a kind of sour brown bread with practically no wheat flour."

Among the prisoners, the Chefoo schoolchildren were probably the healthiest. We had never been used to the luxurious life enjoyed by many in the business community. In our parents' mission outposts, or at Chefoo with simple fare to feed 300 hungry boarding-school kids, we were used to the song "Where he leads me I will follow/ What he feeds me I will swallow."

Singing in Prison

And of course our personal faith in God also made a great difference. I remember a Sunday night in the camp church joining others in singing "Beneath the Cross of Jesus":

I take, O cross, thy shadow for my abiding place,
I ask no other sunshine than the sunshine of His face,
Content to let the world go by, to know no gain or loss,
My sinful self my only shame, my glory all the cross.

The question God was asking me was whether I would be content with "the sunshine of His face" regardless of circumstances. I told God that night that I was content with him, even in prison. This was a turning point in my accepting the daily grind of prison life. Another came one Easter when Mrs. Buist, a Salvation Army missionary from Wales, sang in her powerful clear soprano, "I Know That My Redeemer Liveth." As she stood on that cement slab, she sang hope into my heart with new assurance that my resurrected Lord was alive.

I have often been asked why we sang so much in prison. But that was often the only thing we could do. We couldn't get away from it all for a weekend, or even get a cup of coffee and take a break. Yet we could sing, and sing we did. It might be our own lyrics ("If I had the wings of an angel, from the Weihsien world I would fly"). Or as rumors spread in 1945, we sang to the tune of "O Bring Back My Bonnie to Me":

The Russians have landed in Norway,
Rabaul is reported to be
In the hands of our staunch U.S. allies,
But that sounds like rumor to me!

The guards are all leaving on Wednesday,
And weekend will see us set free,
But look in tomorrow at tea-time,
And there'll be some rumors for tea!

But the greatest music in prison was brought to us by The Salvation Army Band. And no one enjoyed the band more than Mor did. "It is Sunday and The Salvation Army has just played so beautifully outside. It is wonderful to have this freedom in prison," she wrote to Edvard (in response to the first letter that had reached us from him in two years). "The Band gives us such a good Sunday mood as they play the old hymns that Far and I used to sing when we were young. They have horns and trumpets and just play so well to the great encouragement of everyone in camp."

Family Life and Mor's Ministry
In the same letter Mor described the nine-by-twelve room where she and I slept (Hakon and Torje were with the Chefoo boys in the dormitory). My brothers joined us for meals. We fetched our food from

148

the kitchen and warmed it up in the clay stove with an oven, which Hakon had built. Her letter is filled with gratitude to God that we are together. Despite these meager arrangements, Mor was grateful to be with her children and the CIM community. This, she thought, was better than being outside prison and bearing her burdens alone as an isolated single parent.

In his description of the Lunghua Camp near Shanghai, novelist J. G. Ballard hinted at the same type of security a prison can provide. Jim, the young hero of his story, had set pheasant traps outside the camp to supplement a meager diet.

After roll-call that morning he had slipped through the fence. . . . The first of the traps was only a few feet from the perimeter fence, a distance that had seemed enormous to Jim when he first crept through the barbed wire. He had looked back at the secure world of the camp, at the barrack huts and water tower, at the guardhouse and dormitory blocks, almost afraid that he had been banished from them forever.

Of course, prison life had its drawbacks. But in spite of all the hardships, Mor's gratitude to God made her a tower of strength to many others in the prison. Quite a few would come to her for prayer and to share their burdens. As I was on the move most of the time, she could offer them the privacy of our little room. But she was also sensitive to the many who would not come to see her on their own. Therefore she and some other women started the Service Committee, from which people could request help for specific needs or put in a request on behalf of a friend in need. In this way Mor touched many people she would not have met otherwise.

One page of her records survives. There are entries such as, "Dr. Corkey applied to the Serv. Com. to take charge of Di-di whose mother was going to have an operation. Miss Williams, being willing, moved in to their room and stayed with the child for three weeks."

Another child, eleven months old, was cared for by two volunteers during the seven months of her mother's illness. Mor also started "The New Laundry Scheme," from which those too sick or weak to wash their own clothes could get help. As the years in prison dragged on, more and more would require such help. Many gave up trying to take care of themselves or their families, while those with a serving spirit became busier and busier in an effort to save the camp community from chaos.

Mor was also active in the White Elephant exchange, started by her good friend Mrs. Hubbard, who with her husband was among the leaders of the camp from the beginning. It was Hugh Hubbard who wrote what has become the famous "Weihsien Test":

Whether a man's happiness depends on what he has, or what he is; on outer circumstances, or inner heart; on life's experiences—good and bad—or on what he makes out of the materials those experiences provide.

I think Mor passed that test. She found as many opportunities to minister in camp as she ever had outside. Her other commitments included the Women's Auxiliary, for which she visited the sick and lonely, helped overworked mothers with mending and organized a nursery "for wee children's care." While many complained of boredom, Mor was so busy that sometimes I would hardly see her between meals. Even as a prisoner, she was still a missionary.

Langdon Gilkey, in his *Shantung Compound,* was describing people like Mor and Eric Liddell when he wrote,

There was a quality seemingly unique to the missionary group, namely, naturally and without pretense to respond to a need which everyone else recognized only to turn aside. Much of this went unnoticed, but our camp could scarcely have survived as well as we did without it. If there were any evidences of the grace of God observable on the surface of our camp existence, they were to be found here.

The "Bamboo Wireless"

There were 400 Protestant missionaries among the 1,600 prisoners. Just before our group from Chefoo arrived in Weihsien, 400 Catholic priests and nuns had been moved to Beijing, though some remained. One of these was Father Raymond de Jaegher, a Belgian priest with long years of experience with the Chinese. He volunteered for the job of Sanitary Patrol Captain. This gave him contact with the coolies who came into camp to carry out the human waste each day, and with their dedicated help we had a secret channel of news from the outside world. David Michell tells the story:

"No dawdling or talking to anyone," the guard growled as de Jaegher, keeping just out of sight of the guard in charge of the work crew, kept watching his messenger coolie closely. . . . With the guard now round the corner, the coolie turned and, looking in de Jaegher's direction, spat into the dust. . . . De Jaegher . . . picked up the little pellet he could see lying in the dirt. With his heart pounding he went back to his tiny room [and] unwound a piece of tightly folded rubber film to find a small sheet of silk with a typed message on it. . . . There were many close calls, such as the time a guard . . . forced the new coolie at bayonet point to open his mouth. With a gentle gulp he swallowed the pellet, and with it our latest news bulletin! . . . The steady stream of . . . news never ceased in spite of such setbacks. . . . Contact with the world outside kept up morale. The wall had been conquered.

But there was another source of news—the Japanese. At the start of the war we had been impressed with their discipline and respect for authority. But there was a change. Guards were seen walking unsteadily from too much wine, and also complaining about their superiors to people like Edvard's friend Norman Cliff, who was slowly learning their language. One day he and a companion were emptying ashes just outside the gate and talking to the guards on duty. After some small talk Cliff asked, *"Senso- ka o- ari -mashita-ka?"* ("Is the war over yet?")

"Ma-da ooari-masen" ("It is not yet finished") was the reply. Then another guard conveyed in Chinese, Japanese and sign language that when the war was over, all prisoners would be shot and all Japanese soldiers would fall on their swords. Other prisoners heard the same message from the guards, leaving us with mixed feelings about looking forward to an Allied victory.

Liberation

And then it all happened in such a beautiful way. After having heard of the Armistice through the "bamboo wireless," we still had no official confirmation of V-J Day—that is, not until the message came from the blue skies above us. Thirteen years old at the time, Torje wrote the story later at school in Norway:

A little over a year ago I experienced the happiest and most surprising day of my life. On August 17 at 8 a.m. I had been out pumping water. On the way back I thought I heard something, stopped to listen, but heard no more. I walked a few steps and stopped again. From far, far away I heard the sound of planes that didn't sound like Japanese planes. This time I was sure, and started running around the prison-camp shouting, "A plane, a plane." But I was not alone. Suddenly I saw everyone running out of the barracks to look.

There we stood in the still clear summer morning and watched a four-engine American plane coming right toward us. Many men and women watched with tears in their eyes, while others didn't know whether to laugh or cry. I stood there with a big lump in my throat and watched the plane coming nearer and nearer and trying to shout, "Hurrah." Soon it was right above us, and then we started shouting and screaming with all our might. Such homage came

152

from the throats of 1,600 prisoners that I almost think they must have heard it up in the plane.

The plane flew back and forth and came lower and lower, and then the jubilation knew no bounds when red, yellow, green, blue and white parachutes descended from the heavens, and seven men landed outside the camp. The excitement was almost more than we could stand, but I found myself in a big crowd, storming the gate which had been closed for three years. The guards were afraid and ran, and like a wild herd we darted over the plains looking for our saviors. As soon as we found them, the parachutists were hoisted on men's shoulders and carried into camp as heroes while the Band played and we all sang a medley of various Allied national anthems. Without having been a prisoner inside the walls for three years, no one can imagine how wonderful it was to be free again. . . .

Now our liberators took over the camp. One of the Chefoo teachers wrote,

We had a victory supper yesterday. We had a tomato each, and an apple, too! It was almost overwhelming. The morning we ran out the Chinese were shocked at all the bare feet; some picked up children and carried them back. They have also sent in cotton undershirts. The boys and men were shirtless too, and the dear Chinese thought we had no clothes at all. Chinese Christians are coming to the gate all day long bringing us food.

With all the excitement of freedom and plenty to eat, it was not too hard to wait till September 25, when we were allowed to leave the prison. We were now under the Allied military until we were properly repatriated to our homelands. My first question after freedom was "When can we go back to Hequ?" We had hoped we could make a visit to our former home before leaving China. But while one war had ended, the struggle for the control of China had escalated between the Reds and the Nationalists, making travel to Hequ impossible.

The next question was whether to go home to Norway, or petition to go to North America to see Edvard and his new bride, Jenny. When this latter door opened, we were all happy about it and sailed into the unknown—toward the New World—where none of us had ever been before.

Far's and Mor's
Ministry to Mongols
and Chinese Continues

10

After waiting two months for a ship to cross the Pacific, we began our twenty-eight-day voyage. We arrived outside New Westminster, British Columbia, in Canada on the last day of 1945. The ship dropped anchor in the harbor because we could not land until after the New Year's holiday. But when the pilot came out to the ship my brothers, tired of the sea, begged for a ride to shore. Who could refuse two skinny young boys, full of enthusiasm about being the first to step on North American soil?

Hakon and Torje were allowed to roam around the farm country by the pier where the pilot left his launch. They were glad to feel solid ground under their feet again. Torje tells the story of their adventure:

When we strolled into the field we found cows grazing and were curious. We had not seen cows for all the years in Chefoo and Weihsien. And so I walked up to a cow, and tried to grab a teat. I wanted to taste some milk, but the cow got all shook up. Suddenly the farmer from a distance . . . started yelling at me. I got nervous, as he ran across the field towards me, but managed to say, "I just wanted to taste some milk."

"Milk? Where are you from, that you don't get milk?"

"We're from that ship you see out in the harbor. Just came from China where we've been in a prison camp—without milk."

"And who were you with in China?" the farmer asked, and was completely taken by surprise when we said we had been with the China Inland Mission. . . .

"The China Inland Mission! Why, we support the CIM! We go through the prayer book and have been praying through the list of names of missionaries and their children every day," he blurted out, so wild with enthusiasm that he left Hakon and me speechless.

"And now God has sent you from that ship out there right into my field to tell me that my prayers have been answered," he continued[.] "Why here you are alive as I prayed you would be!"

Suddenly he said he had to run and tell the rest of the prayer group that had been meeting at his farm every Friday night during the war—that here was living proof of answer to all their prayers. But then it struck him that there might be more of us on that ship, and after getting all that information, he decided to get the whole CIM crew off the ship for a big celebration. And we could stay in all the homes of those who had prayed us out of prison.

After a complete New Year's thanksgiving in the bosom of our new Christian family for three days, we were taken back to the ship to land properly. The Red Cross met us and drove us to the CIM headquarters in Vancouver, and kindly outfitted us with warm winter clothes. Then we boarded the train for Toronto, where we were reunited with Edvard and met his lovely bride, Jenny.

The Reunion

I wrote in my diary, "After being first greeted by numerous reporters, we at last found Edvard and Jenny." The joyful family reunion was shared with the public through pictures in the next day's papers. And then the catching up started—hours and hours of filling in the story of the silent years when most mail didn't get through. We stayed at the CIM headquarters but had our evening meals at Edvard's and Jenny's tiny student apartment. Edvard was enrolled at Toronto Bible College, and Jenny at the Missionary Medical Institute. They were preparing for their future with the Mongols of China.

In April, when the school term was finished, we moved across the border to discover another new land, the U.S.A. This time it was Jenny's sister's family who opened its home to us. It was impossible after the war to find an apartment for us, so Mor was filled with gratitude for this provision. She had learned never to take family life for granted, but always looked on it as a special gift from God.

We also had the opportuntity of sharing our story of God's love to us through the war. The Norwegian Evangelical Free churches around New York were the ones Far had preached in thirty years earlier— especially the Sixty-Sixth Street Church, where he was ordained. Many people remembered him well, and one told me, "I have prayed for you every day by name." I was amazed. So was Mor. She wrote home to Norway,

This time in Brooklyn and Orange [New Jersey] has been a good time. It has been so wonderful to visit friends in the Free Churches here. . . . All the children have joined me in giving testimony to God's goodness, and at several meetings the whole family has stood up and spoken and God has used it. It has often made a deep impression on people when the children get up and speak about

157

God leading them. Pray that they will be protected and useful in the service of Jesus."

Not too long ago I met a relative who remembers hearing us speak in Brooklyn, "Oh, how can I ever forget your mother coming home from the war and so radiant! And then she had so many children who got up on the platform too to speak. It seemed like there were about eight of you."

We weren't quite eight, but we did have an addition to the family during these months. Mor's first grandchild, Leif Peter, was born to Edvard and Jenny. That meant seven Torjesens were living with the Landruds in their tiny four-room apartment! But not for too long. In June we made the grand exodus. It was then Mor confided how she dreaded going home to Norway without Far. It was like going through the grief all over again. Leaving Norway in 1937, we had been six in number; and now she was returning in 1946 with only Torje (age fourteen). Hakon and I wanted to study in the U.S., and Edvard and Jenny had their sights on Mongolia.

But again, Mor found her strength in turning to God. She found a ministry of sharing, with audiences all over Norway, the story of the war and God's goodness to us. At the same time she ran the Mission Home, boarding a capacity of thirty guests. There she and Torje lived with other missionary families.

Edvard Carries Out Far's Vision

At the end of 1947, Edvard and Jenny came to Norway to say good-bye to Mor and to Jenny's mother before leaving for China. They also wanted to present the needs of the Mongols to God's people in Norway. Mor was delighted that Edvard was carrying out Far's unfinished task. At this time Edvard wrote an article for the mission organ *Kinamisjonaeren*. This was his story of how God had used Far's concern to call him to evangelize the Mongols.

If the power of the Gospel does not touch the Mongols now, another generation will be lost. This was my father's concern when he met Mongols on his visits to Chinese settlers across the Great Wall. I was too young to remember what he said, but after he had given his life for the Lord's work in China, and after I had had a definite call to the Lord's service, then I had this impression that . . . if he could, he would also have given his life for the salvation of the Mongols. If there was anything that hurt Far deeply it was to know that just a little way North of the Great Wall there were eight to ten tribes of Mongols who were without God or hope in this world. . . . Far's concern was that someone would accept the call to bring them the Gospel. . . . For over two years God called me, and not until God's grace was victorious in my life, did I have peace in my heart.

Sailing for China

On September 1, 1948, Edvard, Jenny and little Leif set sail for China. Just before they sailed, their senior missionary told them the opportunities to reach Mongols were greater than ever before. He had a caravan of eight camels and three horses ready for a team to penetrate further into Mongol territory. Edvard could hardly wait.

When they landed in Tanggu near Tianjin, Jenny said her first culture shock was to discover that Edvard was home. While she was checking out the new land, Edvard was talking, in colloquial Chinese, to the people he met on the street. Their senior missionary met them in Tianjin with the news that he had left Inner Mongolia for Ningxia Province due to the advance of the Communists. But there was a five-room inn in Yinchuan, Ningxia, ready for them. And so on the same day the U.S. Marines evacuated most foreigners from North China, this little band of pilgrims flew three-and-one-half hours inland. From Yinchuan they went by car to Gansu Province to study Mongolian.

159

Edvard wrote from an inn en route about all the exciting possibilities that lay before them. After their February baby was born, they could either return to Ningxia Province or penetrate further into northwest Gansu or go into Xinjiang Province. With eight million Mongolian nomads moving about in the steppes of Central Asia, the options were many.

"We arrived here on November 28, Far's birthday, " Edvard wrote to Mor from Lanzhou. With his Christmas greeting he remarked, "This year we [Torjesens] are spread to the four winds of the world." We were on three continents: Asia, Europe and North America. But in spirit we were all with Edvard and Jenny in China, exploring new frontiers to conquer for Christ.

To Edvard's delight his language study was supplemented with trips to explore future possibilities. He and their senior missionary made numerous journeys up the panhandle of Gansu and into Qinghai Province—anywhere the Mongolian caravans would pass through. In Qinghai alone they learned there were 130,000 Mongols divided between twenty-nine tribes. As late as July 25 they were still planning to move to Dulan, west of Xining and Qinghai Hu (Koko Nor Lake), where there were twelve Mongol tribes. But suddenly, because of dramatic developments in China's civil war, this was impossible. Evacuation was in the air, so Edvard and Jenny knew that maybe their days in China were numbered.

A Second Torjesen Grave
But they were not leaving China and the Mongols until they had added one more Torjesen grave to the Chinese soil. Little David was born on February 4 and was usually content and smiling. But when he was three months old he suddenly got seriously ill and moaned with pain. He was examined by a doctor, but died in Jenny's arms.

At the time, Edvard was on one of his exploratory trips into Mongol territory. At first Jenny believed he would be unable to make it for the funeral. But miraculously he arrived early at Zhangye, where the telegram was waiting for him, so he got back on time. David was buried beside five other missionary children. And so David joined his grandfather in China's yellow soil, to await the resurrection.

A few months later the trip to Qinghai was canceled when officials in the Mao regime disapproved of it. Edvard and Jenny wrote later, "With the rapidly advancing liberation army coming closer, there was only one thing for us all to do; to get out. It was a hard decision to arrive at, but when we did leave on August 13 [1949], we knew it to be the Lord's will."

With two Mongolian families, including their own language teacher and other missionaries, they were able to start the Institute of Mongolian Studies on Laan Tao Island outside Hong Kong. There they worked on the revision of the Mongol New Testament and a language study manual for future missionaries. "Pray that in His time we may return to Mongolia," they wrote in September. "In the realm of the Spirit we can win!" They were still determined to keep alive Far's dream.

Mor's Plans for China

The same month that Edvard and Jenny left China, Mor left Norway. She planned to visit Hakon and me in the U.S., then hoped sometime to return to China. She was fully cognizant of the political situation, but still hoping the doors to her beloved Hequ would open again. Then, the following month General Mao Tse Tung announced the founding of the People's Republic of China. And by October 1949 Canton had fallen.

The CIM made the controversial decision that the Mission should remain in China under a Communist government. When Great Britain recognized Communist China they took the recognition as further confirmation of their decision. "Besides—China would not change!" a CIM author wrote. "Down through the millenia the country has survived invasions and political upheavals and remained basically the same. She did not resist her conquerors—she absorbed them! The Chinese will outlive Communism. They appear to yield, but they always end up doing their own things their own way." This optimistic viewpoint gave Mor hope.

Hakon and I were on Chicago's Union Station platform to meet Mor and Torje late that summer. As the train pulled in Mor was her same sweet self, but Torje was no longer the skinny little guy who came from prison camp. He was huge, and with skis in hand he looked to me like a handsome sports hero. We spent a few days with him, catching up on three years apart, and getting him settled at Wheaton College. I had just graduated from Wheaton and was going on to graduate school at the University of Minnesota where Hakon was also enrolled. Hence we had an apartment ready in Minneapolis for Mor and the two of us.

Mor was excited to have a home with two of her children for the first time since 1940, the summer after Far passed away. But she was still a pilgrim, reminding us she was ready to go back to China as soon as possible. She was just as much a missionary now as when Far lived. Her call was separate from his, so there was never any question whether or not she might continue without him. There were those in Norway who tried to discourage her and advised her to settle down to a more comfortable lifestyle. But Mor was not interested. She had a call to be a prophet to the nations (Jer 1:5-10).

As a missionary-prophet she used every opportunity to tell young people that no life can be more exciting than serving the Lord on new frontiers. Ruth Stam Thiagarajan, missionary to Tibet, remembers her that fall of 1949, taking part in the Northwestern College Missionary Conference: "I suddenly noticed this slight woman in a black coat with

162

six young men around her—completely mesmerized by what she had to say. Her face was absolutely radiant. I just had to find out who she was."

Besides speaking for churches and schools interested in missions, Mor discovered there were 200 Chinese students at the University of Minnesota. It didn't take long for the Christians among them to invite her to come and help with a Bible study, using both the Chinese and English Bibles. As the group grew larger, Mor prayed for a bigger home she could open to the many of them, who (like her) were separated from loved ones in China. And so by 1950 God gave us a house that was filled with Chinese students on Sundays.

Open Doors in Taiwan and Minnesota

By 1952 Mor received a call from Taiwan to come and help with the throng of refugees who had fled from the Communists in China. And so at sixty, she embarked for a new land to face a new challenge. That September, I sailed with Mor across the Pacific on the *Flying Dragon,* as I had signed a contract with the National Taiwan University to teach English literature.

On arrival, Mor joined Edvard and Jenny in Pingtung (in the south of Taiwan) where they had moved from Hong Kong to continue evangelism among refugee Mongols. Our first Sunday there we heard Edvard preach in Mongolian. Because he and Jenny were concentrating on the Mongols, but very aware of the needs among the Chinese refugees, they were most grateful to have Mor come and help them. She fit right in—calling herself a refugee from China like the rest of them. After a little more than three years in Taiwan, she had helped to start three churches among the Mandarin-speaking people from China.

But there was a price. Not only was she away from Hakon and Torje during those years, but when I returned to the U.S. after two years in Taiwan and married Bob Malcolm, Mor could not be there. Knowing how hard it was for her to miss her only daughter's wedding, I wrote about the ceremony, "The mother's seat was empty while out in Taiwan, Mor knows the meaning of leaving 'children for my sake and the gospel's.' "

Then, after her sojourn in Taiwan, Mor returned to Minneapolis. There she busied herself with her Chinese Bible study, which had developed into a church, and was having a growing ministry among students and professionals. Also waiting for her was Torje, ready to introduce his Norwegian wife, Reidun. After time in the military, Hakon too returned to Minneapolis and—still single—decided to buy a house for Mor and himself in 1957. Again she looked on a home as a blessing. Chinese students continued to visit her there, and many knelt at the sofa of this home and received Christ into their lives. She was a mother to them emotionally and spiritually—and formally at their weddings—as well as grandmother to all their children. (In addition to her Chinese grandchildren, she soon had Hild and Rolf, Torje and Reidun's children, also in town to enjoy.)

Thirty years later I still meet Chinese families who knew Mor and called her Mother. The Twin City Chinese Christian Church has grown to number more than 300 and have its own building. It was my privilege recently to introduce Pastor Joseph Wong as speaker at a conference. I was happy to share my joy that he pastors the church that started as a Bible study with my mother's help.

Mor's Last Trip to the Orient

Because of her missionary calling, Mor was on the opposite side of the Pacific when three of her children were married. Now Hakon turned the tables, and instead of getting married in the U.S., decided to have a Taiwan wedding, with brother Edvard and brother-in-law Bob (my husband) officiating. So Mor decided it was time for a trip to the

Orient—to get in on the last wedding in the family!

Mor was seventy when she flew across the Pacific and visited Bob and me in the Philippines just before the wedding. We were missionaries in student work at the time, and she was full of stories about her Chinese students. Before Mor came, we had just heard at a student conference that an ideal student worker should not be over thirty, and relayed this to her.

"Oh, no," Mor said, "It has nothing to do with age, but with the heart. Do you love the students?" She had no intention of quitting student work and continued until she was seventy-three, forty years past the "ideal" student worker's deadline.

While she was with us, she thoroughly enjoyed her grandchildren, Kirsten and O-i (Lois). We also had her speak to churches and groups, including the Ministerial Fellowship. She spoke radiantly of the goodness and faithfulness of God. After a few war stories, she was back again to her favorite: "Oh, but God is so good to us even in the worst circumstances. The secret is God, who is with us."

"I've never heard anything like it," a missionary told me later. "After all she's gone through, yet she only has praise for God who allowed it all, and is so thankful for all his goodness and mercy."

As her daughter I knew Mor was as capable of getting discouraged as anyone else. But then she would take a morning (or afternoon or night) in prayer and pour out her heart to God. Then would follow the comfort of the Holy Spirit, like soothing oil on her inner wounds, and God would speak just the right word to her through the Scriptures, or directly into her thoughts. And Mor would be newly encouraged.

After this visit, we flew with Mor to Hakon and Karen's wedding in Taiwan. We had a grand time, with Edvard's six children and my two all in the wedding party. It was a family affair and Mor enjoyed it to the full, especially being with her grandchildren. After the wed-

165

ding, Mor and I took a sentimental trip to Hong Kong, the only place from my China childhood open to us. We relived our stops there: 1936 and 1937, when we lived there as refugees; 1938-1939, when we waited for the ship after World War 2; and 1954, when Mor and I enjoyed a visit. Then I put her on the plane for Laos to spend some time with Hakon and Karen at their home. (Hakon was in Laos working with the U.S. Information Agency, a public relations arm of the government.)

Invigorated, Mor returned in the fall of 1962 to her Chinese congregation in Minneapolis. By the time Bob and I returned to Minneapolis in 1964, she had just broken her hip. In that big hospital bed, she seemed to have shrunk since I last saw her. She looked like a little bird. Caring for God's birds was, in fact, how she had broken her hip. She had stepped out with food for them on a cold morning and slipped on the icy steps.

Later, with Mor rolling around in a wheelchair in her home, I asked her about the yellow bird attached to one of her plants. She told me how there was nobody around to celebrate her anniversary, so she called the florist and ordered a special plant. Although she had not told him it was her anniversary, or that her husband was gone, he sent her this plant with a lonely yellow bird. To her it was God's message that although she was alone, she could continue to sing as long as she lived.

Mor Retires

We had a wonderful furlough year with Mor, and when we were going back to the Philippines, she was ready to retire. She spent the following winter with Edvard and Jenny, who were on furlough in New Jersey. From there she went home to Norway, in time for the annual conference of the mission. There she was honored for her forty-five years in active ministry to the Chinese people. She also gave her last public talk, a final paean of praise.

When we came to Norway in 1967 and 1970, Mor was in a wheel-chair due to another hip fracture. We saw Tante Thora, and she told us how much she enjoyed her visits with Mor. Of course they re-hearsed their wonderful years of bringing the gospel to Hequ, as well as the trials, and they prayed together. But one day Mor had made a remark that made Thora both laugh and cry:

"Well, Thora, do you think we have to go back to China?"

"Oh, no," said Thora, "I think we have done our part and God is satisfied with that."

"Oh, that's good to hear. I agree with you. I don't think we have to go back anymore."

Mor had come to terms with her unfulfilled dream of returning to Hequ. Finally it was all right not to go back to a place where she had given so much.

The director of the Lutheran home she was in was a devout Christian and told me repeatedly what a rich inner life Mor had: "She does not need outside stimulation. She is living her own inner life with God." Other residents of the home had only vacant stares, but Mor was in communion with God. While her memory failed her toward the end and she could get times and places confused, when she prayed or talked about the Lord she was fully present. She lived with the Lord where time and place were irrelevant.

This timelessness continued until the end of Mor's journey home on December 12, 1970. The director of the home wrote to me in the Philippines, which eased the pain of not being there:

I sat and held her hand throughout the afternoon. She was quiet and peaceful. I sang some psalms and hymns when I sat there hoping that their message would reach her. . . . She breathed quiet-ly and lay with closed eyes the whole time, until her heart stopped beating at 6:50 p.m. There was a wonderful peace about her and

167

we sat with her the whole time. . . . There is a big empty space after her. For me it is like losing a dear friend. It is good that you were here in the summer and that Hakon was just here. And I think she had you all so close to her heart that the separation because of distance was not so great. She lived her own rich inner life where you were all present.

Edvard flew to Norway to conduct her funeral. It was over fifty years since Mor had signed away her life as she left for China in 1920, willing to live or die that the Chinese might have life. Like Far, she had honored her Lord. Mor and Far had both run the race well, finished the course and kept the faith. Now both brave pilgrims were home at last, where

Those who are wise will shine like the brightness of the heavens, and those who lead many to righteousness, like the stars for ever and ever. (Dan 12:3)

Postlude

Coming back to Hequ, the Song of the River, was the greatest experience of my life. Something had been missing for half a century. I had been cut off from an important part of my roots. Out of touch with the Chinese people who cared for me and played with me, as well as the place that cradled me as a child. So the return was a real homecoming, giving me a sense of inner wholeness. The Song of the River was humming in my heart again.

Forty-eight years after Far was laid to rest near the banks of the Yellow River, we arrived back in Hequ. Dr. Zhang kept her promise and had all the necessary permits ready for us when she met our plane in Taiyuan, the capital of Shanxi. Happily, she told us she would come with us on the adventure to Hequ.

I wrote in my diary February 4, 1988:

"This is the day that the Lord has made, let us rejoice and be glad in it." Off at 7:30 a.m., through towns like Jinglo where Mor lived before marriage, then desert-like regions with knots of dry grass and a few sheep, and more of the sandy hills I remember so well. Entered Hequ along the Yellow River on a paved road after eight hours—instead of eight to ten days by mule! Upon arrival, celebration dinner with seven city fathers. Discovered Lao Quan through his son, the county governor. He had been our goatkeeper and was identified with laughter and joy in my photo album.

The governor grabbed the album and laughed heartily, "Look, that's my father!" He went on to tell us his father still reads the Bible, prays and sings hymns, and always tells him he must get right with God, or he will go to hell. All this was said with great ease and pride before his companions. The fact that his father had been our goatkeeper was also spoken of positively. Such an immediate connection with my past underlined my certainty that I was really home.

The second day I woke up with a full heart. Was I really in Hequ? It was another exciting day, one of talking non-stop for thirteen hours. First Lao Quan arrived, saying, *"Ma-li-a laila!"* ("Kari has arrived"). He was full of stories about his happy years with us. He was delighted to see his picture in my album, as well as that of Pastor Nie of Hequ, now a pastor in Inner Mongolia. Now 73, he talked of the day our house was bombed, referring to my father with his Chinese name Ye Yong Ching (Evergreen Leaf) or Ye Mu-she (Pastor Leaf), and calling my mother Ye She-niang (Mrs. Leaf).

"Ye Mu-she was a good man," he continued. "When I was sick he cooked medicine for me. He stayed with me three days and three nights. He bought me a fur coat because I was cold. I had pneumonia and no appetite."

Then Lao Quan took us to Swei Chao Go (Water and Grass Ditch), the location of Far's grave. It was now in the middle of a cultivated field, but a well-known spot to the neighbors. They knew exactly where it was because they were there when the marker and fence around the gravesite were removed. I was prepared for this, as I had read that with one billion people to feed, China could not spare fertile land for the dead. But it was still a bit of a shock, as the picture I had in my mind was what Mor and Tante Thora had described—a quiet setting in the field of the farmer who donated the space. In the spring and summer, they had said, a garden of flowers bloomed around the grave, which was carefully enclosed by a neat wooden fence. On the gate leading into this garden, the carpenter had asked Mor if he could place a cross, as Far always talked about the cross.

Without this nostalgic setting, it was good that Edvard's daughter, Jean Valborg, had made a lovely ceramic bowl to be placed on her grandfather's grave. The Hequ officials had the best calligrapher in town inscribe on it, *"Ye Yung Ching Zhe Mu"* ("The Grave of Evergreen Leaf").

Many neighbors gathered around the grave and three older men said they remembered Ye Mu-she well. They were among those who identified the spot where he was buried. A woman my age arrived and said she was my former *"wang gwa"* (playmate).

After our time around the gravesite, and visiting in the home of a neighbor, we went to Lao Quan's house for *chaotze,* or *bientze,* as we call Chinese dumplings in Hequ. The governor and the entire Quan clan were there. After eating a delicious meal, Lao Quan got his well-worn Bible and hymnbook out, and we sang together and talked of the Lord. Though my Chinese was limited, I had a sense of oneness with the old man, to a degree I often do not have with those I can verbally communicate with easier. Lao Quan truly is a man who has walked with God. He told us how he had spent nine months in a re-education camp to clear his mind of Christianity.

171

After dinner, Lao Quan took us to our old house, or what was left of it. He identified one roof section and one window, a section of the house still as it had been in my childhood. It was the storeroom where we kept those boxes of grapes in sawdust during the winter. And the pond outside our gate was there, just as I remembered it. The well was also there. Then we walked to the site of the church, which was also bombed by the Japanese. Whether or not the old buildings were there, I was singing in my heart all the time, "We are standing on holy ground."

Walking around the old neighborhood, we met three old men who remembered our family and blessed Ye Mu-she's memory. When we got back to our hotel, the visitors continued coming until 9 p.m. One of them was my former playmate, who came with her son. She told us her uncle was a Christian, and sent her son to fetch him. He was 82 and, upon arrival, full of memories: "Ye Mu-she came to ask if we wanted to join the church. And Ye She-niang treated my brother for his goiter. But my father didn't join the church. During the Cultural Revolution the authorities came to check on me. I told them I had done nothing wrong—just been healed of my sickness." Then he added wistfully that I was "very filial" to my father. "But my sons and grandsons are not loyal to me because I am a Christian."

The Song Beyond Hequ

On February 6 we headed for the Huang He (Yellow River), where we played as children. Because the river was frozen, we were asked if we wanted to walk across into Inner Mongolia. So we entered the area that was my father's dream for the expansion of the gospel.

I wrote in my diary later,

It hit me—right in the middle of the river—that God is using the church from Hequ and Pastor Nie [Far's key man] to reach the Mongols. First it was Edvard, and now these precious Hequ Christians who have probably known a persecution and a scattering similar to Acts 1:8, "A great persecution arose against the church— and they were scattered throughout the region." Praise God for using this old method.

Before this moment of truth in the middle of the river, I had wondered what had happened to the Christians. Why did I only meet a few? The explanation offered was that the younger Christians had left for Inner Mongolia, where there are now 20,000 residents from Hequ County. There are only 120,000 people left in Hequ County, and 10,000 in Hequ city, the same number as there were during the bombing in 1939. While the population in the rest of China has more than doubled, Hequ has not grown.

Later we were also told of the church growth in Inner Mongolia. In the city of Baotou (130 miles north of Hequ and well known to my folks) there are ten registered churches and 100 house churches. There were 1,000 baptisms in the last year. This is also the fruit of my parents' labor, it came to me clearly. Their gospel song, which had merged with the Song of the River, had penetrated Inner Mongolia many miles beyond Hequ.

The church growth in Inner Mongolia is also reflected in a statement by researcher Jonathan Chao: "During the last 40 years the church in China has grown from less than one million to 50 million in spite of, or perhaps because of, the persecution." Similar good news comes from David Barrett, author of the *World Christian Encyclopedia.* He has said that the church growth in China has been greater than any church growth in the almost 2,000 years since the expansion of the New Testament church. I thank God that my parents had a share in adding to those statistics.

As I pondered such things on the frozen river, I thanked God for giving me part of the answer to a question I had often asked: Why did I have to lose my Far, just when I needed him most, at fourteen? And

Edvard at fifteen? Hakon at eleven? And Torje at eight? Of course we will not understand such mysteries until we reach heaven, but then I felt as if I got a glimpse of the answer. I had new evidence that when Far was killed, he did not die in vain.

Witnesses in Hequ

Later, in my warm bed at the hotel, I had other questions for the Almighty. There were probably house churches in this area, but we weren't certain. So what about Hequ? Why couldn't there be a church here, as in other parts of China? I wasn't ready to believe that Far's death had not lastingly touched Hequ. Everything else seemed well, but that no Christians would gather on Sundays to sing praises in Hequ was distressing.

Before we had retired that night, one of our visitors at the hotel was Dr. He Ling, who was the director of the County General Hospital, housed in an impressive building. Hequ had come a long way since Mor's clinic was the only medical center in this part of Shanxi. Dr. He identified his grandmother in my photo album, and talked about how she prayed every day and continued in her faith. And then he concluded, "Nobody ever said anything bad about your parents."

As he said it, I remembered that we had heard that before as news trickled out from Hequ during the early days of the Communist take-over. When those who had been associated with missionaries were accused of imperialist connections, the Christians in Hequ had said, "Evergreen Leaf was not an imperialist. He came from the little country of Norway and lived and died among us and was always just one of us."

Now I was hearing the same thing forty years later. Gradually the talks we had enjoyed three evenings in a row with city leaders were beginning to gel. Over and over they would say, "We are in our forties. Even though we never knew your father, he is part of the town's

174

history. We have heard what he said and did from our elders."

It began to dawn on me that the Holy Spirit was continuing a living witness of the shepherd who had come to them. This living witness, passed on from generation to generation, is reinforced by the grave. Far's grave was the sharp, underlining symbol of his love and dedication to these people. When during the Cultural Revolution Bibles were burned, churches closed or turned into warehouses, and pastors and lay Christians killed or imprisoned, Far's grave remained a homily that could echo his love for the people of Hequ. Nobody can silence a grave.

While Hequ didn't have a visible church, it had something nobody could remove during the darkest days of the revolution. The marker had been removed, but everyone knew where the grave was. Nobody had forgotten the shepherd who had stayed of his own will, suffered and died with them, and been buried among them. The rest of us had left Hequ, but Far in a sense never had.

Then I began to see the answers Mor never saw. She reached her heavenly home before she made it back to Hequ, and was blessed for believing without seeing (Jn 20:29). But to me was given the privilege of seeing the answer to my questions with my own eyes.

On our last morning in Hequ, as we were driving out of town, I longed to stop one more time to see the grave. But I knew Dr. Zhang was eager to move, as our permit had already expired. So I struggled with the emotions of years welling up within me. I glanced in the direction of the grave as we passed and, choking with tears, said under my breath, "Good-bye, Pappa."

Honoring Evergreen Leaf
Another part of the answer to my question—why I had to lose my father at fourteen—came a few months after we left China. Hakon and Karen went to Hequ in June (not in February with us) because Dr.

Zhang had invited them to assist her in a medical seminar at that time. By June the city officials of Hequ had decided to build a monument in honor of Peter Torjesen, so Hakon and Karen received the official invitation for the Torjesen family to come to the ceremony of unveiling the monument. What an honor for Far, and for the Lord he served, to be saluted by a secular state. (The full text of the inscription for the monument is given in Appendix 1.)

We are in the process of setting the date for the ceremony, a little over fifty years after Far laid down his life for Hequ. Our hope is that the four of us and our spouses, and as many children and grandchildren who are able, will join Hequ in honoring Evergreen Leaf, for "great is the LORD and most worthy of praise; . . . One generation will commend your works to another; . . ." (Ps 145: 3-4). In Hequ, we will praise God for his works, remembered and passed down from generations past.

So who is being honored as a brave soldier of the cross is honored? Glory is brought to the Lamb who was slain as the followers of the Lamb go to their death willingly.

As one CIM veteran put it,

God himself is seen as the Lamb Who died to redeem. They [his followers] died in making him known, at his command. . . . To all eternity we shall live and reign with Christ, but shall we ever be able to make sacrifices for him again? When sin and pain and death are no more, and all tears are wiped away, shall we ever have again the privilege that is ours now of sharing the fellowship of his sufferings "to seek and to save that which is lost"?

I have finally caught the note of triumph in those words. Those of us who lost Far had the privilege of entering into Christ's sufferings for Hequ and Inner Mongolia, an honor believers will not enjoy through eternity. I really didn't lose a father! The way he died and the reason he chose to risk his life, gave me a hero and model for life, a father who never stopped speaking to me in his own loving way. The suffering I have known has been assimilated in the greater cause, the goal of giving away the gospel, that grippped Mor and Far.

Far caught a glimpse of that privilege and honor when at seventeen in Norway he signed his life away for China with the binding words "And my life." This promise was renewed when he and Mor left for China and signed the statement that they were willing to die for the cause of bringing the gospel to China. And once again, they signed their lives away when they decided to stay and suffer and be willing to die with the people of Hequ. So it is that one day we will hear the singing of the redeemed from the Song of the River blending with the celestial chorus:

Hallelujah! Salvation and glory and power belong to our God, . . .

Hallelujah! For our Lord God Almighty reigns. Let us rejoice and be glad and give him glory! (Rev 19:1, 6-7)

Appendix 1

Translation of the Chinese text prepared for Peter Torjesen's monument in Hequ:

Pastor Ye Yung Ching was born in 1892 in Norway. Right from childhood he gave himself to Christianity, and when he was grown up, he was always looking to the East, especially admiring China, and longing to spread the good news to the people of China.

In 1918, when he was 26 years old, he arrived in China. Three years later, he chose Hequ as his parish and from then on he did rescue work during famine and provided medical services and education for the people. He contributed a great deal to the local people and rooted himself in the friendship of the people.

Blessed is the man who trusts in the Lord . . .
He is like a tree planted by the water,
That sends out its roots by the stream,
And does not fear when heat comes,
For its leaves remain green,
And is not anxious in the year of drought,
For it does not cease to bear fruit."
Jeremiah 17:7-8 [Chosen for its reference to the evergreen]

His decision was to go down by root and go upward by fruit, and that was his motto. And that was the reason for his Chinese name, Ye Yung Ching (Evergreen Leaf).

This man worked industriously and honestly the whole of his life. He declared peace and humanity, and never got tired. He was against the war of invasion, so when the Japanese invaders came to China, Mr. Ye sympathized and helped the Chinese soldiers and the civilian people during the war. Regretfully this support was reported by spies. He was killed on December 14, 1939 during a sudden bombing of an organized group of planes—dive bombing—and bombing the church. At the age of 47, he died for China. He served the people. He ardently loved China. He served a great deal to help the people. He really died in the anti-Japanese war. Therefore, we erect a monument here in memory of him at the place facing the Yellow River and the plateau of Hequ. We recognize his spirit in heaven. His spirit is immortal.

Appendix 2

Letter from a German Catholic priest in Hequ, sent to Valborg on the anniversary of Peter's death, translated from the German:

Peace and Blessing!
Our esteemed Reverend Mrs. Torjesen,

My heartfelt condolence on the anniversary of your husband's death to you and your children. Please send my regards also to his father and extended family. We honor the brave who fall in combat for their homeland. However, when a missionary sacrifices his life, then all of us, in spite of grief, share a sacred joy. Pastor Torjesen stood in the frontline as God's soldier, bearing the pains of battle, and gaining an immortal crown of victory. Wait a little while, then you will all meet again, with no more separation. May your husband's task and sacrifice of life contribute to our dear God's shortening of these days of war's visitation, soon granting the entire world peace.

Again my kindest regards to the children. May they become as pious and brave as their father.

With cordial greetings,
Father Prosper Luber

Chronology of Events

(Political events are italicized.)

1766-1122 B.C.	*The Shang (Yin) Dynasty flourishes in the Yellow River valley, where Chinese culture began (around the time of Moses).*
255-206 B.C.	*The Qin (Ch'in) Dynasty, which gave China its name, produces its first emperor. He links together the 1500-mile Great Wall.*
A.D. 1840-1842	*The Opium Wars, with the West forcibly opening China to foreign trade and gaining rights for inland navigation and, later, missionary activity.*
1892	Valborg Tonnessen and Peter Torjesen are born in Kristiansand, Norway.
1900	*The Boxer Rebellion*
1911	*Revolution overthrows Manchu Dynasty, ending 3600 years of dynastic rule in China. Sun Yat-Sen declared president of first Chinese republic.* Peter leaves Norway in February, to prepare for missionary service at the Norwegian Evangelical Free Church Bible School in Rushford, Minnesota.
1913-1916	Peter takes the three-year course at Moody Bible Institute and goes on to Northern Baptist Theological Seminary. Returns to Norway and enters the military.
1914-1918	*World War 1*
1916-1918	Valborg enters nurses' training in preparation for missionary work. With Peter back in Norway, they get engaged. They are accepted as missionary candidates to China.
1918	Peter sails for China.
1919-1920	Valborg has a year of Bible school, followed by the China Inland Mission Candidate School. She sails for China.
1921	Peter opens a new post for the gospel in Hequ, where the Great Wall and the Yellow River meet.

1921-1923	Valborg fulfills the required two-year language course before marriage.
1923	Peter and Valborg are married in Shanxi.

1927   *Chiang Kai-Shek leads anti-Communist coup. Mao leads peasant uprising.*

Due to the unrest, 5,000 Protestant missionaries leave China. The Torjesen family returns to Norway for furlough.

1928   *Chiang Kai-Shek establishes order through the Kuomintang—a nationalist one-party dictatorship.*

With conditions improved in China, the Torjesens return to China.

1928-1935   In Hequ and beyond, years of revival.

1936-1937   The Torjesens furlough in Norway.

1937   *Japan invades China in July.*

1937   In spite of war, the Torjesens leave Norway for China. Since Shanxi is already in the conflict, Valborg and the four children go to the Norwegian school in Hunan, while Peter unsuccessfully tries to achieve Hequ alone.

1938   Early in the year, Peter reaches Hequ. As the Japanese advance toward Hunan, the Norwegian Missionary Society decides to evacuate the school to Hong Kong.

1939   At the end of the school year, the Norwegian school-in-exile closes. The Torjesen children transfer to China Inland Mission school in Chefoo, Shandung.

1939   Peter journeys from Hequ to join the family for a summer in Chefoo.

World War 2 begins in Europe.

The four Torjesen children are left in Chefoo, and Valborg and Peter return to Hequ.

Peter dies at age 47 in a Japanese bombing attack.

1940   Valborg stays in Hequ to shepherd the Christians through the crisis of losing their church, much of their town and their pastor. She returns to her children in Chefoo that summer.

1940   *Germany invades Norway in April. The Norwegian government in exile in England joins the Allies.*

1941   *Pearl Harbor is bombed and all citizens of Allied nations are under Japanese arrest.*

1942	The China Inland Mission school and all Allied citizens in Chefoo are marched off to prison camp.
1943	All the Chefoo prisoners, including the Torjesens, are transferred to Weihsien, where 1,600 prisoners are confined until the end of the war.
1945	The Torjesens and other prisoners are liberated by the Allies and begin the journey to North America.
1946	In June, Valborg and Torje return to Norway, while Hakon and Kari stay in the U.S. to study. Edvard and Jenny prepare to reach the Mongols in China.
1948	Edvard and Jenny leave for China to carry out Peter's unfinished task of evangelizing the Mongols.
1949	Political and military events force Edvard and Jenny to evacuate China to Hong Kong, where they help start the Institute of Mongolian Studies.
	Valborg and Torje arrive in the U.S.—Torje to go to college, and Valborg hoping still to return to Hequ after visiting her children in the U.S.
	The Chinese People's Republic is proclaimed in Beijing.
1950	Valborg starts Bible studies with Chinese students from the University of Minnesota.
1952	Edvard and Jenny have moved to Taiwan to continue work among Mongols, and invite Valborg to assist with Chinese refugees.
1956	Valborg returns to her Minnesota Chinese Bible class, which has become a Chinese church.
1966	After retiring from Chinese student work at age 73, Valborg goes back to Norway to live. She is honored by the mission for 45 years of faithful service to the Chinese people.
1970	Valborg dies at age 78.
1988	The door to China reopens miraculously, and four members of the Torjesen family return to their hometown of Hequ.
1990	Hequ prepares a monument to honor Peter Torjesen, fifty years after he was buried there.